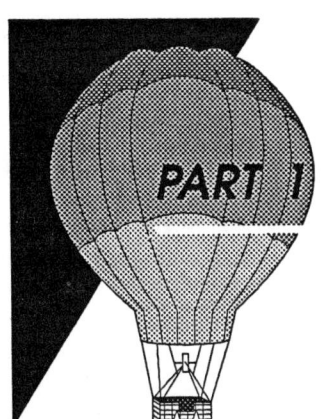

PART 1 *GETTING STARTED*

chapter **1** ▶

Introduction to Unix

A major problem with any book on the UNIX operating system is where to start, especially because the UNIX operating system is so large. The UNIX System V Release 4 (SVR4) version of UNIX contained approximately 12 million lines of source code and documentation. Most versions of UNIX now require an entire bookshelf for just the hardcopy documentation. There are approximately 50 separate manuals for the UNIX operating system. This makes the task of creating a comprehensive book with examples and exercises almost impossible. However, selections from the author's favorite set of commands and tools are provided to help the user quickly master the basics of the UNIX operating system. The following subjects are discussed in this chapter:

- Basic terms
- UNIX shell and **login**
- Basic shell exercises
- Changing directory locations
- Listing files
- Creating and editing files
- Removing files
- Quoting characters

1.1   BASIC TERMS

Before we discuss how to get started with UNIX, it is important to first discuss some of the many terms that are used throughout the rest of this text.

The *operating system* is the software that manages the hardware devices associated with the computer system. UNIX is an operating system that was developed back in 1969 at Bell Labs by Dennis Richie and Ken Thompson. The operating system provides instructions for all hardware devices, for example, the central processing unit (CPU), memory, hard disk, and other devices.

The UNIX *kernel* is the operating system itself. The kernel is the software required for the computer (hardware) to perform basic operations such as reading the disk or writing text characters to a display device. The kernel is responsible for managing memory, allocating system resources, maintaining the file system, and controlling access to the system. Many of these functions are provided by specific software modules called *device drivers*. These device drivers are incorporated into the UNIX kernel and are usually transparent to the user.

A *process* is a program during execution. UNIX is a multiuser and multitasking system, so there can be many programs or processes that appear to be running on the system at the same time. A multiuser system provides the ability for more than one user to utilize the resources of a single computer system. A multitasking system allows each user to have many processes or programs. Even though UNIX is a multiuser and multitasking operating system, only one process actually is able to execute or run at a given moment. However, because of its speed, it appears that many users and processes are able to run concurrently.

The *scheduler* is the process responsible for scheduling or managing which program will run. Remember that the UNIX operating system is a multitasking and multiuser operating system, therefore, it is important that the scheduler provide some amount of time for each and every process to execute.

A *signal* is a method of communication between processes. This is also sometimes known as an Inter Process Communication (IPC) mechanism. Users are able to send signals to the UNIX kernel to perform specific processing functions. For example, to terminate a process, the user can use the control and C keys together to send a SIGKILL (terminate) signal to a process. You can use the UNIX **stty** command to display the default signal and terminal control handling settings.

A *shell* is a program that provides an interface to the UNIX operating system. The shell is a command interpreter because each user command must be interpreted by the shell before it is passed to the kernel. The carriage-return key is used to dispatch all shell commands. A collection of shell commands can be located in a special executable file called a *shell script*.

A *file* is simply a collection of information or data that is normally stored on the hard disk. Almost everything in UNIX can be considered a file, including each and every device associated with the computer system, for example, disk, memory, video display, floppy, tape, and keyboard. All UNIX device files are located in the **/dev** directory.

1.2 THE UNIX SHELL AND LOGIN

The UNIX shell is the command interpreter that allows users to communicate with the operating system. The shell is an interpreter because it takes each command input that is terminated by a carriage return and processes the requested command. However, before users can expect to obtain access to the UNIX shell via a prompt, they must first successfully log in into the UNIX system. The log in process requires an account name and an associated password that is stored in a system-specific file (**/etc/passwd**). The first exercise we must always perform with the UNIX operating system is to log in to the system. Follow my example below on your system by typing in a valid UNIX log in name and password. If you need help with an account (log in name) and password, see your system administrator. You must successfully complete the following exercise to complete all other exercises.

In the following example, I type in the string "rodney" as my log in name and complete the input with a carriage return. Next, the **login** program calls the UNIX **passwd** program that presents the password prompt. Once I type in my correct password, the UNIX system presents a shell prompt. In the following example, my shell prompt is a percent sign. This is the standard prompt for the UNIX C shell. If the prompt were a dollar sign, "$", that would indicate that I was using the Bourne shell or Korn shell. If the prompt were a pound sign, "#", that would indicate that I was logged in as root or the system administrator (in most cases).

login: rodney
passwd:
Welcome to the UNIX system
%

Notice that when you type in your password, your keystrokes are not displayed on the screen. This is so that your password remains secure (no one can see the characters that comprise your password). Usually you should never share your account or password with other users. The text displayed after successful log in prior to the percent prompt is contained in the **/etc/motd** file. This file contains the message of the day (**motd**). The **motd** file is most useful for servers where multiple users are sharing disk devices. For example, if you have critical data on

a public server and you want to make sure that the disk is not formatted or removed, include this information in **/etc/motd** to inform other users (especially root) after they log in to the system.

Exercise 1

1 Stop at this point and enter your log in name and password.

2 Identify which shell you are running as the Bourne shell, C shell, or Korn shell.

---

logout and exit

Once you have complete your work with the UNIX shell, it is always recommended to use the **logout** or **exit** command. This is good for security reasons, because once you have logged into the UNIX system, anyone else can use the keyboard until you log out. The **logout** command returns the UNIX system to the **login** prompt.

1.3   BASIC SHELL EXERCISES

Once the user has access to the shell, commands can be entered for processing. The first command that we explore provides information regarding our current directory location on the UNIX system. The UNIX file system stores both files and directories in a hierarchical structured file system. This is the same structure as is used in a company organization chart. For example, there is always a company president at the top followed by vice presidents, directors, managers, and, finally, other employees. This UNIX file system structure is also called a tree structure with the top of the tree called the root. It is sometimes more helpful to draw a picture of an organization and turn the picture upside down. The root then is on the bottom and the leaves on the top.

Because the UNIX file system is a hierarchical-based system, it is sometimes easy to get lost. Therefore, the system provides the command **pwd** to print the working directory or current directory location. Use the following example to print your current working directory.

```
% pwd
/usr/rodney
```

In this example, my directory location is under the **usr** directory in a subdirectory called **rodney**. When you first log in to the UNIX system, the user is always located in their **HOME** directory. The **HOME** directory is specified by the system administrator when the user account is first created (stored in the **/etc/passwd** file). This directory must be owned by the user, otherwise files and subdirectories cannot be created by the owner of the account. However, more about permissions and ownership will be provided shortly. Now, try the following exercise to print the current working directory.

Exercise 2

1 Assuming you are still logged into the UNIX operating system, enter the command to print the current working directory.

2 Identify the parent directory name.

1.4   CHANGING DIRECTORY LOCATIONS

Once you have identified your current working directory or location in the UNIX hierarchy, you may want to change to a new directory location. As you will begin to notice, all UNIX commands have names that are abbreviations for the function that they perform. For example, the change directory command is **cd**. As you witnessed in the previous section, the command to print the current working directory is **pwd** (print working directory). The majority of all UNIX commands are abbreviations for the functions they perform.

The following example changes my current working directory to a new location (the **tmp** directory) by using the **cd** command.

% **cd /tmp**

Notice that the UNIX shell, by default, does not provide any output as a result of executing the **cd** command. However, if I had specified a directory location that did not exist, it would have complained with an error message, as shown in the following example:

% **cd /doesnotexist**
/doesnotexist: No such file or directory

In this case, the directory **doesnotexist** really does not exist. Therefore, the shell cannot change my current directory location to this directory.

It is important to point out that when changing directories with the **cd** command, there is a difference between *absolute* and *relative* paths. The two examples preceding show how to change directories using an absolute path name. An absolute path name always starts with a "/" or from the root of the UNIX file system. Remember earlier that I said that the root is like the president of the UNIX file system and is at the very top of the hierarchy. When we specify a directory name that starts with "/" or from root, it is absolute because it must start from the root or top of the UNIX file system. Conversely, relative paths start from the current location. In order to explain relative paths, we must first explain the purpose of two very important *hidden files* that are located in each UNIX directory. These two files are called "." and ".." and are considered hidden because they are normally hidden from our view when we look at the contents of a directory. More will be said about hidden files in the next section.

The file "." is pronounced *dot* and is used to identify the current working directory. The file ".." is used to identify the parent working directory. Therefore, the ".." file in the directory **/usr/rodney** points to or is really only a reference to the directory **/usr**. As an example, if my current working directory is **/usr/mnt** and I want to change to the parent directory or **/usr**, I can simply type the following at the UNIX shell prompt:

% **cd ..**

Exercise 3

1 Stop at this point and use the **cd** command to change to the **/tmp** directory using an absolute path.

2 Next, use the **cd** command to change to the **/etc** directory using a relative path from **/tmp**.

3 Explain the basic difference between an absolute and relative path.

4 Can you think of any advantages or disadvantages of using absolute vs. relative paths?

1.5   LISTING FILES

Now that we have discussed the print working directory and change directory commands, let us explore how to view the contents of a directory. The **ls** command lists the contents of a directory. Without any command-line options or arguments, we only see a list of names using the **ls** command. If you do not have any data in your current working directory, you will not see any output from **ls**. You can create an empty file using the **touch** command. See the following example for how to create an empty file using the **touch** command in a directory that is currently empty:

```
% ls
% touch myfile
% ls
myfile
```

Notice that the command **ls** did not present any data until I used the **touch** command to create a new file **myfile**. The **ls** command has many other options and possibilities that will be discussed later.

Exercise 4
Use the **ls** command to list files in your current working directory. If you do not have any output from the **ls** command, use the **touch** command to create a new file as indicated in the previous example.

By the way, the **touch** command also can be used for files that already exist. In this case, the date and time stamps for when the file was last created or updated are changed to reflect the current date and time after using the **touch** command. You can verify that the date and time stamps for a file are updated by using the **touch** command on an existing file by using the -l option to the **ls** command. This command checks the date and time, as shown in the following example:

```
% ls -l
-rw-r--r--  1 rodney                  0 Aug 23 17:58 myfile
% touch myfile
% ls -l
-rw-r--r--  1 rodney                  0 Aug 23 17:59 myfile
```

Notice that the time (Aug 23 17:58) changed by 1 minute after the second execution of the **ls** command.

1.6   CREATING AND EDITING FILES

Now that we have been able to list files, change directories, and print our current working directory location, let us look at how to create and edit files using the UNIX **cat** and **ed** commands. The easiest way to create a file in UNIX is to use the **cat** command or **cp** commands. Let us start with the **cp** command because it is the simplest to explain.

To copy an existing file, you simply need to specify an existing file name and the new file you want to create (as an exact copy). However, you must separate the existing file name and the new file name using the space character. This is a very important character, which is also called a *delimiter*, because it separates commands, arguments, and file names. In other words, provide the ability for the shell to break a command into tokens or individual components (command-line arguments).

The following command copies a file in our current directory, called **myfile** (created in the previous section using the **touch** command), to a new file called **newfile**.

% **cp myfile newfile**

If the file **myfile** did not exist, then the copy command would have failed because it could not make a copy of a nonexistent file. Even though the **cp** command does create a file, we are only creating a duplicate of an existing file, rather than an original.

The next command, **cat**, allows the user to create an original file from scratch. However, before we discuss the **cat** command, we must first explain a concept called *redirection*. The UNIX shell by default opens three very important file descriptors after log in to the system. The first file descriptor is assigned the number zero to represent input. This file is usually associated with the keyboard connected to the computer and is also called *stdin*, or *standard input*. The next file descriptor, or file number is assigned the number 1 and is for output. Output by default is always assigned to the display device or console device connected to the computer. This is also called *stdout, or standard output*. The third file descriptor is assigned the number 2; remember, we really started from the number zero (which is very common in UNIX). This file is opened after log in for error messages and this file is also associated with the display device (by default). This file descriptor is called *stderr, or standard error*. By using redirection from the shell, we can change any of these defaults for input, output, and error data. For example, if I would like my output from the **ls** command to be sent to a file called **myoutput** instead of the display screen, I simply need to use the greater-than sign, ">". The following example sends the output of the **ls** command to a file instead of the display screen (default output device):

% **ls > myoutput**

Notice that the contents of the directory are not displayed on the output device any longer, because the output is now stored or redirected to the file **myoutput**. If we want to write data directly from the keyboard to the file called **myoutput**, we can type the following (one of the fastest ways to create a new file using the UNIX shell):

% **cat > myoutput2**
this is my input from the keyboard that will be
stored in the file myoutput2
^D

Notice that the input must be terminated by using the control and D keys together. This is a special key sequence that tells UNIX that this is the End Of File (EOF) input. Now we can use the **cat** command to display the contents of the file **myoutput2** using the following example:

% **cat myoutput2**
this is my input from the keyboard that will be
stored in the file myoutput2

You will notice one major difficulty associated with using the **cat** command along with the greater-than sign, ">", to create a new file; the problem is that once you have completed a line with a carriage return, the previous line cannot be changed or edited. This is because once we enter a carriage return, the data from the keyboard are sent directly to the file. Therefore, an editor is a much more efficient way to create a new file. One of the most basic editors associated with the UNIX system is a line editor called **ed**. The **ed** editor is very similar to the DOS **edlin** editor for making changes on a line-by-line basis. Examples are often the best way to explain how to use a UNIX command, so let us start with the following example. One creates a new file using the **ed** editor. This is followed by adding data using the **a** command. Next, we will display the contents of our file by printing from line 1 to the end of the file with the command **1,$p**. Finally, we need to use the **w** and **q** commands to write our data to the file and quit the **ed** editor.

% **ed newfile**
a
this is new text that I am creating the file
I will need to enter a period "." on a line by itself to
terminate input
.
1,$p

this is new text that I am creating the file
I will need to enter a period "." on a line by itself to
terminate input
w
q

The **ed** editor provides other basic functions for deleting lines and substituting characters using the **d** and **s** commands. The following two commands first delete line number 1 using the **d** command after first positioning to line number 1. Next, we change the text on the current line (old line, now number 1) to replace the letter "I" with the string "We". Finally, we print the entire contents of the file **newfile** using the command **1,$p**. Don't forget, we always need to either use the commands **w** followed by **q** or **q** and **q** to quit without saving our changes.

% ed newfile
1
d
s/I/We/
1,$p
We need to enter a period "." on a line by itself to
terminate input
w
q

We cover the **ex** and **vi** editors in later chapters. As you will see, these editors build upon the features of the **ed** editor and provide even more features for data modification (text editing).

Exercise 5

1 Use the **ed** editor to create a file with a text message that explains the basic commands we have just discussed for adding and deleting lines.

2 Include text that describes the command to substitute one word of text with a new word.

3 Finally, in the body of your document using the **ed** editor, explain the commands to write your changes to the file and quit the **ed** editor.

1.7   REMOVING FILES

The **rm** command allows the user to remove a file from a directory. The **rm** command requires the user to specify the file name as part of the command syntax. Therefore, just typing **rm** without a file will do nothing, because a file name target was not specified. The following example removes the file created in the previous exercise for using the **ed** editor:

% **rm newfile**

You can confirm that the file **newfile** has actually been removed by using the **ls** command in the current working directory. The results of the **ls** command must show that the file is no longer available, unless you do not have write permission for the file. (You must have write permission to a file in order to remove it from the directory.)

% **ls**

Exercise 6

1 Use the **touch** command to create a new file and use the **rm** command to remove the same file name.

2 Verify that the file has been removed using the **ls** command.

3 What happens when you attempt to remove a nonexistent file?

4 Create a file again in your current working directory and this time remove the file using the complete (absolute) path.

1.8   QUOTING CHARACTERS

The UNIX shell provides the ability to treat some characters as special characters. These characters are also sometimes called **metacharacters** because they provide many meanings. For example, the character "?" says that we can

match any single occurrence of any character. If you want to list all files in the current working directory that start with the letter M and end with the letter D separated by one character, use the following:

% **ls M?D**

If we want to create a file that contains an actual question mark as part of the file name, we must use another special character to help escape the special meaning of the question mark. We can use the double quote characters to protect against the shell from interpreting the special meaning of the question mark. For example, to create a file called **?mark**, we need to perform the following:

% **touch "?"mark**

To verify that the command has been created properly, we can use the **ls** command again, as follows:

% **ls**
?mark

The "\" character also can be used to escape the special meaning of the question mark. Place the "\" character right before the special character (i.e., ?). To remove a file with an embedded special character (e.g., ?, *), we need to use the same rules that were applied to the creation of the file. We must surround the special character with the double quote character (or preface it with a back slash) to avoid removing all files that contain the string "mark" after the first character.

% **rm "?"mark**

To verify the results of the **rm** command, use the **ls** command to display the new contents of the directory. The other wildcard or metacharacter that is commonly used is the asterisk. This character is like the question mark; however, it represents one or more occurrences of any character. Remember, the question mark only represents a single character position, whereas the asterisk can represent multiple occurrences. If we want to list all files that contain the string "ant", we can use the asterisk before and after the string, as follows:

% **ls -a *ant***

.   ..   pant   scant   scanty.txt

Notice that this command also matches files that contain a file extension (**scanty.txt**). However, hidden files (**.ant**) are not displayed unless a period is placed before the asterisk, as follows:

% **ls .*ant**
.ant

You must use the **-a** option to the ls command to see all files contained in a directory. By default, the **ls** command does not show files that start with a period (hidden files). These files are commonly used to define rules and definitions for a program (e.g., **.profile** contains settings for the Bourne shell and **.vacation** contains text for the **vacation** program and the entries for dot and dot dot were discussed previously).

% **ls -a**
.

..

.profile
.vacation
pant
scant
scanty.txt

Exercise 7
1 Use the double-quote characters to create a file using the **touch** command that is called **?special_file.**
2 Next, use the **rm** command to remove the file that was just created.
3 Create the files **spring, fling,** and **wing.**
4 Use the **rm** command to remove just the file **wing** using the special metacharacter.
5 Explain the difference between the question mark and the asterisk during these operations.

chapter 2

Communication and File-Handling Tools

*T*he UNIX operating system provides a number of useful tools for communication user-to-user and program-to-program communication. In this chapter, we provide exercises and examples for using commands to **write, talk,** and **mail** users information. The following programs are discussed in this chapter:

- Who is on the system? (**who**)
- Writing data to users (**wall**)
- On-line manual pages (**man**)
- The **echo** command
- What day and time is it? (**date**)
- Moving files (**mv**)
- The line printer (**lp** and **lpr**)
- Searching for a string (**grep**)
- The **head** and **tail** commands

- Sorting data (**sort**)
- Differences between files (**diff** and **sdiff**)

2.1 WHO IS ON THE SYSTEM?

The **who** command allows the user to review what users are logged into the UNIX system. This command is very simple to use, simply type **who** followed by a carriage return and the system responds with results that list all users currently logged into the system.

% **who**
rodney console Aug 1 13:59

Notice that the results of the **who** command include not only the user name, but also the device used for log in and the date and time when the **login** program was first executed. The **who** command is more useful for servers or big systems where many users log in. The **rwho** command is useful to determine who's logged in on local machines connected to a Local Area Network (LAN).

Exercise 1

1 What command displays the users that are currently logged into your UNIX system?

2 Use the redirection symbol (discussed in the previous chapter) to store the output data in a file on disk instead of sending the output to the screen display device.

2.2 WRITING DATA TO USERS

The **write** command allows a user to write a message to another user that is currently logged into the same UNIX system. Because this is an intrusive command or can disrupt other users, an additional command is provided as a supplement to the **write** command. The command is **mesg**. This command allows message notification to be turned either on or off depending on the user's prefer-

ence. By providing an "n" after the **mesg** command, the user turns off the message notification. Therefore, if someone attempts to either write or talk to the user, the request will be denied. Message notification is always on by default after log in. This is the same as providing a "y" after the **mesg** command. See the following examples:

```
% mesg n
is n
% mesg y
is y
% mesg
y
```

Notice that the last command without an option simply shows our current message setting or the current default. It is often a good idea to keep message notification turned on, as this is the only method that the UNIX system administrator has to notify the user of important events, such as system shutdown.

To write information to users that are logged in, use the **write** command followed by the user's log in name and a carriage return. You must then type in text that you want to write to a specific user. If you want to write to a user that has logged in more than once, the **write** command will send data only to the console log in window for the user by default (this only occurs if you are using the X Windows system). Alternatively, one can specify a specific display device for users that are logged in more than once. You can use the **who** command to identify the port for the user that you want to use for **login** and specify this after the user's name. See the following example for how to use the **write** command:

```
% write rodney
write: rodney logged in more than once ... writing to console
This is my message I type in....
^D
% who
rodney ttyp1 Aug 10 12:59
rodney ttyp2 Aug 10 12:59
% write rodney ttyp2
Message from rodney@cds9407 on ttyp2 at 13:52 ...
This is my message to rodney on ttyp2
^D
```

As is the case with the **who** command, the **write** command only sends a message to users located on the same local machine. If you want to **write** to all remote users logged into machines connected to the same network use the **rwall** command (you must be running the **rwalld** to use this command successfully). Expect a performance penality for starting either the **rwhod or rwalld** system processes.

The **mail** command is probably one of the most important and frequently used tools with the UNIX operating system. Electronic mail has become one of the most economical and efficient methods of communication possible (often less expensive than phone or fax communications). Many companies are now located throughout the world and rely heavily upon electronic communications. Therefore, electronic mail has become even more important for proper communication between groups, organizations, and companies.

The **mail** command is very simple to use. The following example sends electronic mail to a user called **rodney** with a subject line and one line of mail text (assuming that our PATH looks in **/usr/ucb** before **/bin** to obtain the BSD **mailx** and not System V **mail** program). It is important to notice that the text is terminated by using the control and D keys together. The text message can also be terminated using a single period on a line by itself. A carbon copy or "cc", line is then displayed for other users to which you can send copies:

```
% mailx rodney
Subject: Test Mail
This is the body of my message.
^D
Cc:
```

Once we have sent mail, we naturally want to read any new mail that has been received. In this case, because we sent mail to ourself (rodney), we can simply use the **mail** command again without any options to check for new mail. In the following example, you will notice that we have one new message in our mailbox from rodney with the subject line of "Test Mail". The date and time of the message are also provided. After the number "1" is typed at the "&" **mail** prompt, the message contents are displayed:

```
% mailx
>N1 rodney Wed Aug 24 16:48 14/430 Test Mail
& 1
Message 191:
From rodney Wed Aug 24 16:48:19 1994
Return-Path: <rodney>
Received: from cadence.Cadence.COM by cds9407 (5.65+/1.5)
 id AA18240; Wed, 24 Aug 94 16:48:18 -0700
Date: Wed, 24 Aug 94 16:14:56 -0700
From: rodney (Rodney Wilson)
```

```
Message-Id: <9408242314.AA15958@cadence.Cadence.COM>
Received: by cadence.Cadence.COM (5.61/3.14)
 id AA15958; Wed, 24 Aug 94 16:14:56 -0700
To: rodney
Subject: Test Mail
Status: R
& s mailfile1
& q
```

Typing the letter "s" followed by a file name saves the current message on the disk with the name as specified. Typing a "q" at the prompt causes the **mail** program to remove the message from the system-wide mail folder and store the message in a private mailbox called **mbox** in our home directory. Remember the home directory is automatically assigned by UNIX from the **passwd** file after **login**. We can reopen our private mailbox using the "-f" option to the **mail** program.

If there is no unread mail, then the system will respond accordingly. Because we have just completed reading all of our mail and if we now attempt to open the systemwide mail folder, will find that no mail exists. We can use the **biff** command followed by the "y" option to turn on notification of mail messages, instead of continuing to check for mail. The following example shows what happens when we attempt to read from an empty systemwide mail folder:

```
% mailx
No mail for rodney
```

Exercise 2

1 Use the command to send a test **mail** message to yourself.

2 After you have completed sending the **mail** message, open and read your mail.

3 After you finished reading your mail, save the mail message to a disk file called **mymail**.

4 Use the **ed** editor to delete the mail header and place a ">" at the beginning of each existing line (this is useful when responding to an existing message).

2.3 ON-LINE MANUAL PAGES

The UNIX system has many commands, so it is often very helpful to have reference information readily available for a specific command. The UNIX **man** command provides the ability to read UNIX documentation on-line. For example, if you are not sure about how to use a particular command, one can give the command name in question to the **man** command. In the following example, we are interested in more details regarding the **ls** command:

% **man ls**

If you are not sure about what command you need to use to perform a particular function, use the **man -k** command followed by a string. In the following example, I have requested a list of all the commands that have to do with the keyword "search":

% **man -k search**
acctcom (1)   - search and print process accounting files
bsearch (3)   - binary search a sorted table
grep, egrep, fgrep (1V) - search a file for a string or regular expression
hsearch, hcreate, hdestroy (3) - manage hash search tables
lsearch, lfind (3)   - linear search and update
tsearch, tfind, tdelete, twalk (3) - manage binary search trees

If you receive an error message as a result of attempting to execute this command, it is probably because the **man** command's database that holds all the information on each command has not yet been built. This is often the case because the database does require additional disk space; however, the database can be build fairly easily. Simply use the **"catman"** or **"makewhatis"** command to build the database. You normally will also need to be the system administrator to create the special **whatis** database file.

Exercise 3

1 Use the **man** command to obtain on-line manual information about the **man** command.

2 What are two commands you can use to obtain on-line manual (**man**) information about all commands that have to do with "searching"?

2.4   THE ECHO COMMAND

The **echo** command by itself may not seem very useful at first. The purpose of the command is to echo data to the screen or output device. However, when the command is combined with a shell variable, it can be very useful. All UNIX shells provide the ability to create local variables. For example, we can create a variable name that stores the contents of our user name by using the **set** command using the C shell, as follows:

% **set username=rodney**

In the Bourne shell, the **set** command is not needed to assign a value to a variable. To perform the same function using the Bourne shell, type the following (must type "sh" to start the Bourne shell):

$ **username=rodney**

Now using the **echo** command, we can display the contents of the variable **username** as follows (regardless of the shell we are using):

$ **echo $username**
rodney

It is important to note that we now use the name **$username** with a dollar sign to identify that we want to display the contents of a variable, rather than an actual name. Otherwise, if we simply provided **username** to the **echo** command, it would echo the string "username" as follows (assumes that we have started a C shell by typing "csh", or exited from the preceding Bourne shell using the **exit** command):

% **echo username**
username

Exercise 4

1 Use the **echo** command to show the difference between a string literal with your first name and a variable that contains your last name.

2 Create a variable name called "student" and assign the variable the value of your first name. Next, use the **echo** command to display the contents of the variable as well as the variable name.

2.5   WHAT DAY AND TIME IS IT?

The UNIX system must know the date and time for many reasons. One important reason is because when you create a file, for example, using the **cp** command, you often want to know when you last made the copy of a specific file. Having a date and time helps you to know if the file is up to date with the latest version of the original source file. To display the current date and time, you simply need to type the following:

% **date**
Wed Aug 24 18:00:34 PDT 1994

Notice the string "PDT". This says that our time zone is based upon Pacific Daylight Time. UNIX also uses military time, therefore, 18:00 is really 6:00 P.M. Make sure you do not confuse the **date** command with the **time** command. The **time** command provides information about how much time it took for a command to execute. Therefore, if you just type "time", you may end up with a funny result that might look like the following:

% **time**
12.4u 37.4s 50:29 1% 0+244k 7018+197io 6754pf+0w

Instead, you should use the **time** command with a command prior to execution as follows:

% **time ls**
myfiles
0.0u 0.0s 0:00 66% 0+128k 2+0io 1pf+0w

The **time** command shows the amount of user and system time. Another way of explaining this is to find out how much time the UNIX kernel took to run vs. the amount of time our program (**ls**) took to execute. In this case, the execution time was less than a second. You can use the **man** command for the **time** command to obtain even more details for how your system reports system execution time.

Exercise 5
What command displays the date and time on your system?

The **touch** command is used to create a file. If the file already exists, it will

update the date and time when the file was previously modified or created to the current date and time.

The UNIX **sleep** command causes the current process (program under execution) to sleep the number of seconds provided after the **sleep** command. For example, **sleep 1** causes the shell to do nothing for 1 second and then returns the shell prompt.

Exercise 6

1 What command creates a new file?

2 Use the **sleep** and **time** commands together to verify the accuracy of the results provided by the **time** command.

2.6   MOVING FILES

Earlier, we discussed the **cp** command to copy one file name to another. This makes a duplicate copy and keeps the original. However, if we wanted to remove the original file and only keep the copy, then we should use the **mv** command. The **mv** command moves the file name. Another way to think of this operation is to rename a file or directory from one name to a new name. The following command changes the file **newfile** to **movedfile**; notice that no output is provided as a result, only the shell prompt:

```
% mv newfile movedfile
% ls newfile
newfile not found
```

Exercise 7

1 What command renames an existing file?

2 Can you use this command to rename a directory?

3 Does the directory have to be empty?

4 Create an empty file, rename the file, and verify that the old file has now been removed using the **ls** command.

5 What happens if you attempt to move a file to itself?

2.7   THE LINE PRINTER

UNIX allows users to print to a line printer by specifying a file name after the **lp** (System V) or **lpr** (BSD) command. For example, if you want to print a file on the line printer called **myfile**, simply type the following if you are using a System V based UNIX system (use **lpr** for BSD):

% **lp myfile**
request id is 6

You should notice a message similar to the message that indicates the job number of the print request that was created by the line printer spooler. The print spooler may have several print requests in the **queue**. A printer queue is simply a list of files to print that are pending. The structure used is also known as first in first out, or FIFO. A FIFO, or queue, is just a fancy name for a structure that is the same as a line you wait in every time you go to a restaurant, for example. When you enter the restaurant, usually you must place your name on a waiting list. The waiting list is a queue, or a FIFO.

The **lpq** command (for BSD systems) or **lpstat** (for System V systems) shows all currently active print requests in the print queue.

Exercise 8
1 What command prints a file to the line printer? Give an example for both BSD and System V systems.
2 What commands display the contents of all jobs in the print queue (BSD and System V)?

2.8 SEARCHING FOR A STRING

As you add more and more files to your directory, it becomes increasingly more difficult to remember what file contains the data that you need. For example, if I have created several status reports, I cannot remember which file contains information for the month of November. I often need a way of searching the contents of each file for the string "November". UNIX provides the **grep** command for this very purpose (searching for strings). The following example searches all files in the current working directory for the string "November":

% grep November *

The asterisk is very important because it is a metacharacter that says all files in the current directory. "November" is the string that we want to search for in all files contained in the current working directory. If there are no files in the current directory that contain the string "November" as data, then the command will simply return our shell prompt. However, if there is a match, then each file name will be printed followed by the line that evoked the match, as follows:

% grep September *
myfile: September is a good time for travel.

Notice that in this case, the **grep** command displayed the file name followed by a colon and the line where the match occurred. This only occurs when multiple files are given as input to search from (in this case, the asterisk was used to specify all files and directories in the current working directory).

Exercise 9

1 What command searches all the files in your current working directory for the string "The"?

2 If you have more than one string that you want to search (e.g., the day), what special characters should surround the search strings?

2.9 THE HEAD, TAIL, AND WC COMMANDS

Many times you have large files in your UNIX directory. In some cases you may wish to view only the top or the bottom of a file. To perform this function you can use the **head** and **tail** commands. The following example shows the 10 lines (by default) of a large file called **bigfile**:

% **head bigfile**
this is line 1
this is line 2
this is line 3
this is line 4
this is line 5 (fingers and toes)
this is line 6 (an incomplete number)
this is line 7 (complete number)
this is line 8
this is line 9
this is line 11 (ha ha just fooling!)

To view the bottom of a file, simply use the same syntax as the **head** command, only this time use the **tail** command, as follows:

% **tail bigfile**
this is line 1000
this is line 1001
this is line 1002
this is line 1003
this is line 1004
this is line 1005
this is line 1006
this is line 1007
this is line 1008
this is the last line

The **wc** command is used to display the number of words for a file. By default, the **wc** command displays the total number of lines, words, and characters in the file. This is a quick way of identifying a large file. The **-c** option specifies character counts. The **-w** option specifies words only and the **-l** option specifies lines.

% **cat myfile**

Hello.
How are you?
What is your name?
% **wc -c myfile**
40 myfile
% **wc -w myfile**
8 myfile
% **wc -l myfile**
3 myfile

Exercise 10

1 What command views the top 10 lines of a large file called **big**?

2 What command views the bottom 10 lines of a large file called **big**?

3 Create a large file and verify the number of characters, words, and lines using the word count command.

2.10 SORTING

Many of the UNIX commands provide output data (i.e., **ls, cat, grep**, etc.), so it is often desirable to sort output data. By sorting output in a meaningful form (according to your requirements), raw data can quickly become useful information. The UNIX **sort** command provides the ability to sort data in a variety of fashions. The following example takes the file **foobar** and performs a **sort** of the output in ascending order. However, first we use the **cat** command to first display the original contents of the file:

% **cat foobar**
abcdefg
Rodney Wilson
UNIX exercises
UNIX examples
% **sort foobar**
Rodney Wilson

UNIX examples
UNIX exercises
abcdefg

Notice that the default ascending **sort** command places uppercase characters before lowercase characters. The **-nr** options will provide reverse numerical sorting.

Exercise 11

1 What command reorders data contained in a file that you have created using the **ed** or **cat** command?

2 What command reorders the data contained in a file called **bigfile** with the largest numbers listed first? Create a file with several lines of numbers to ensure that you are presented with lines that contain the largest values first, followed by smaller values in ascending order.

2.11 DIFFERENCES BETWEEN FILES

Oftentimes, you may end up with several files that contain many different versions of the same original file. For example, one may create a monthly status report using your favorite UNIX editor. You may want to know what was performed differently between one monthly status report and the other. For example, what was different between the May and June status reports? Use the UNIX **diff** command to display file differences. The example shows how to identify differences between two files using the **diff** command. First, the contents of the two files:

% **cat may.status**
Status report for Rodney Wilson
I worked hard on the foobar function and gak subsystem.
Increased code coverage for the franastat routine to 90%.
% **cat june.status**
Status report for Rodney Wilson
Created a new design for the blech routine.

Increased code coverage for the blap routine to 90%.

% diff may.status june.status
2,3c2,3
< I worked hard on the foobar function and gak subsystem.
< Increased code coverage for the franastat routine to 90%.

> Created a new design for the blech routine.
> Increased code coverage for the blap routine to 90%.

This example shows that both files contain the same data for the first line, however, lines 2 and 3 are different. The less-than sign, "<", shows the contents of the first file (may.status) that is not included in the second file. The greater-than sign shows the contents of the second file (june.status) that is not included in the first file. Another useful version of the **diff** command is called side-by-side differences, or **sdiff**. The **sdiff** command shows line-by-line differences between two files using the <, >, and | characters. If a line is located in the first file specified on the command line, but not in the second, a < sign will be displayed before the output. The > sign is used for the reverse condition (i.e., in the second file, but not the first). If a line is different but exists in both files, the vertical bar, or pipe symbol, will be used. In the following example, the second line in file **a** is missing from file **b**, the fourth line is different in both files (capital D vs. lowercase d), and the seventh line in file **b** is missing from file **a**:

```
% sdiff a b
aaaaaaaaaaa                          aaaaaaaaaaa
bbbbbbbbbbb            <
ccccccccccc                          ccccccccccc
DDDDDDDDDD             |             dddddddddd
eeeeeeeee                            eeeeeeeee
FFFFFFFFFFF                          FFFFFFFFFFF
                      >             GGGGGGGGGGG
HHHHHhhhhhh                          HHHHHhhhhhh
```

Exercise 12

1 Create two files (**a** and **b**) that contain the pre-ceding data.

2 Use the **diff** command to show the differences between both files.

3 Use the **sort** command and redirect output from file **a** to a file called **c**.

4 Now use the **diff** command to compare both files (**a** and **c**). Notice the change in results when the files are provided in reverse order to the **diff** command.

5 What happens when you use the **diff** command with the same command (i.e., **diff a a**)?

6 Use the **sdiff** command to compare file **a** with **c**.

7 What are some potential benefits of the **sdiff** command over the standard **diff** command?

chapter 3

Files, Directories, and File Systems

*T*he UNIX file system, as was mentioned in Chapter 1, is a hierarchical-based file system. This means that it is organized very much the way an organization chart looks for most companies. At the top of the UNIX file system is the "/", or root, directory. From this directory, other subdirectories or files can be created. To boot (start) the UNIX system, the root file system must be mounted (made available for user access) by the system administrator. The root file system by itself has just enough files to bring the system to a single-user state. When UNIX is in the single-user mode, only the system administrator can use the system (i.e., only the console device provides a **login** prompt). Also, during the single-user mode, no file systems other than the root are mounted and networking services are usually not active. In order for UNIX to run in the multiuser mode, the **/usr** file system must be mounted by the system administrator using the **mount** command. The **/usr** file system contains files that are necessary for multiuser access to the computer system. File systems can be mounted automatically by placing an entry in the **/etc/fstab** (BSD UNIX) or **/etc/vfstab** (SVR4 UNIX) file.

In this chapter, we discuss several commands necessary for file, directory, and file system operation. The following topics are discussed:

- Removing and making directories
- Removing directories with data
- Changing permissions
- Linking files

3.1 REMOVING AND MAKING DIRECTORIES AND PERMISSIONS

To create a new directory, use the **mkdir** command followed by a directory name. Directory names can start with letters or numbers (special characters are not recommended). The **mkdir** command creates a new directory as a subdirectory in the current working directory (unless a path name proceeds the directory name). The following command creates a subdirectory in the current working directory called **mydir**:

% **mkdir mydir**

To create the directory **mydir** under the **/tmp** directory, place the path name (**/tmp**) before the new directory name. For example:

% **mkdir /tmp/mydir**

To verify that there is now a subdirectory in the current working directory or **/tmp** called **mydir**, you can use the **ls** command, as follows:

% **ls**
mydir
% **ls /tmp/mydir**
/tmp/mydir

The **ls** command alone does not really help prove that we have created a new directory. We could use the **cd** command, but that changes our directory and we just want to verify that we have created a directory. A better way of verifying that **mydir** is really a directory and not just a plain text file is to use the -l option of the **ls** command, as follows:

```
% ls -l
total 5
drwxr-xr-x      3      rodney              512 Aug 25 14:55 .
drwxr-xr-x      3      rodney              980 Aug 25 14:55 ..
drwxr-xr-x      2      rodney              512 Aug 25 14:55 mydir
```

Notice that the long listing provided by the **ls -l** command shows much more information other than just a name. The first column of output provides permission modes for each name. The first character listed is a "d" for a directory (regular files would just contain a minus, "-"). The characters after the "d" represent user permissions. Each "r" is for read permission; "w", write permission; and "x", execute permission. These letters are repeated in sequence three times. This is because the first three characters after the file type represent owner permissions (the owner of the file can read, write, and execute). The second set of permissions represents group permissions (members of the group that the user rodney belongs to can read and execute). Finally, the last set of three characters represents permissions other than the owner and members of the owners group (everyone else or "other"). The minus, "-", means that the permission is not available. In the example, only rodney can write to the current working directory (.), parent directory (..), and **mydir** directory. It is important to note that you must have execute permission for a directory in order to use the **cd** command to change to that directory.

The next command, **rmdir,** allows the user to remove directories. However, the user must have write permission to the directory for **rmdir** to honor the request. Also, the directory must be empty before it can be removed. For example, the **rmdir** command does not allow us to remove our currently working directory because we just created a subdirectory called **mydir**. We can remove the subdirectory **mydir** using the following example:

% **rmdir mydir**

To confirm that the directory has been removed, use the **ls** command again.

Exercise 1

1 What commands make a directory in the current working directory?

2 After you have created an empty subdirectory, can you use the **rmdir** command to successfully remove the directory?

Exercise 1 *(Continued)*

3 What happens if you try to remove a directory
without write permission?

4 What happens when you try to create a file in a
directory that does not provide you with write
permission?

5 How about read permission?

6 What happens if you attempt a **cd** to a directory
without execute permission?

7 Attempt to remove a directory that is not empty
and verify the results. Why do you think that
UNIX does not allow users to remove directories
that are not empty?

3.2   REMOVING DIRECTORIES THAT HAVE DATA

One way to remove a directory that is not empty is to change directories
to a subdirectory and use the **rm** command to remove the contents of the directory.
Next, you must change directories back to the parent directory. Now you can
remove the empty subdirectory. For example:

% **cd mydir**
% **rm .***
% **cd ..**
% **rm mydir**

Notice that the **rm** command is provided ".*" as an argument. This is to
make sure that all files that start with a period (hidden files) are removed in the
current working directory. When you execute this command, you get the following
message:

rm: cannot remove `.' or `..'
rm: cannot remove `.' or `..'

This is because you are located in the **.** directory. Also, it is forbidden to remove the parent directory **..** as this could result in a complete removal of a directory hierarchy.

Another more efficient method is to use the recursive option with the **rm** command. The recursive option is provided by using **-r**. This option starts at the very lowest subdirectory in the directory hierarchy and starts removing files. The process continues by moving up one level until you reach the current working directory. The following example removes all subdirectories under and including the directory **mydir** (be careful with this option!):

> % **rm -r mydir**

3.3 CHANGING PERMISSIONS AND THE USER MASK (UMASK)

As was mentioned earlier, UNIX uses read, write, and execute permissions as a basis for program and data security. Each file and directory in the system is assigned an owner and group during creation. The owner of the file has the ability to change permissions for any members in the group or members not in the same group (also known as other users). The command to change permissions in UNIX is called **chmod**. This command changes the mode or permissions for a file in either one of two ways (octal or symbolic notation). In other words, the user can use octal numbers or alphabetic symbols to set file permissions.

To use characters, you simply need to specify the type of permission you want to add or subtract, and for what class of users (i.e., owner, group, or other). The following command changes the permissions for the directory **mydir** by adding read access for the group and write access for others:

> % **chmod g+r,o+w mydir**

The results of the **chmod** command can be verified using the long list option of the **ls** command, as follows:

> % **ls -al mydir**
> total 2
> drwxr---w- 2 rodney 512 Aug 25 14:55 .
> drwxr---w- 3 rodney 512 Aug 25 14:55 ..

The other approach to changing permissions is to use the octal representation. This is a numbering system similar to base 10, except only eight numbers are represented, zero to seven. The best way to describe this method is to use examples.

First, remember that there are three classes of security in UNIX: owner, group, and other. Second, within each class, permissions are always specified by read, write, and execute. Execute permission always is 1, write 2, and read 4. If you want to give execute only permission for everyone including yourself, use the following command:

% **chmod 111 myfile**

In a like manner, if you want to give read and execute access to everyone, use the following (add the value for read and execute together 1 + 4 = 5):

% **chmod 555 myfile**

The process continues in a like manner for changing other permissions as well. The next example shows how to set read and write access for yourself as the owner; however, execute only permission for users in the same group and no permission to others:

% **chmod 610 myfile**

The user mask (**umask** command) is used to define the default file permissions. The **umask** command subtracts permissions (read or write) when the file is first created (assumes a text file that normally does not need execute permission, as is the case with a binary executable). The way you can determine your current user mask is as follows:

% **umask**
22

This is the typical user mask for most UNIX systems. You can only subtract read, write, and execute permissions from a file protection mask. The execute permission is always subtracted when new text files are created. However, if a C program is compiled, the execute permissions will be masked using a **umask** of 111. (We discuss compiling a C program in a later chapter.) The preceding user mask always removes write permission for other users and users of the same group. If the **umask** were 222, write permissions would also be removed, by default, for the owner of the file. The following example shows how to change the user mask so that read and write permissions are not provided (by default) when a file is created (i.e., everything is subtracted):

% **umask 666**
% **touch foobar**
% **ls -l foobar**
---------- 1 rodney   0 Apr 7 09:13 foobar

Conversely, the following example does not subtract any permissions (other than execute for a text file) when the file is created:

```
% umask 000
% touch newfile
% ls -l newfile
-rw-rw-rw- 1 rodney      0 Apr  7 09:16 newfile
```

The next example only removes write permission for users in the same group and read and write permissions from other users:

```
% umask 026
% touch newfile2
% ls -l newfile2
-rw-r----- 1 rodney      0 Apr  7 09:18 newfile2
```

Exercise 2

1 What commands have we discussed so far that allow you to create a file?

2 Change the permissions for the file you just created so that everyone can read, write, and execute the file (use the octal method).

3 How can you verify your changes to the file's permissions?

4 Now change the permissions so that only you (the owner) can read and write to the file.

5 Finally, change the permissions so that you have read, write, and execute permissions, however, group and other users only have read access to the file (use the symbolic method).

6 What command changes your default file permissions for new files to no read or write permission by members of the same group and others?

3.4 LINKING FILES

One common problem with UNIX systems is that over time many system and user files can grow very large. This results in less and less disk space. One alternative to copying a file is to use a **link**. A link is simply a pointer to a file, rather than a complete copy. In general, if many users need access to a single file for reading, a link is often better than a copy or duplicate file. A link keeps all other users up to date with the latest version of the file, without the need for each user to make a private copy. This is especially important if the source or reference file is expected to change frequently, as each user would then be required to make a new copy each and every time the source file changed. Because a link is just a pointer or reference to the original file, it only requires the minimum amount of disk space.

The following command creates a link to an existing file using the **ln** command. This is essentially the same operation as a copy using **cp**; however, disk consumption is greatly reduced. It is also important to point out that the order of arguments or tokens for the link operation is the same as for the **cp** command. The existing file (source) is always on the left and the new file (copy or link) is always on the right. The following command creates a new file called **hard_linkfile** that is a *hard link* to the existing file called **myfile**:

% **ln myfile hard_linkfile**

A *hard link* can only be created within the same file system (mounted partition). In the previous example, both the original file and the link are in the same directory, so a hard link can be created without a problem. However, the following example shows what happens if you attempt to make a hard link across file systems (i.e., from **/usr** to **/usr1**):

% **ln /usr/myfile /usr1/s_linkfile**
ln: /usr1/symbolic_linkfile: Cross-device link

To solve the preceding problem, you must specify the **-s** option along with the **ln** command. This creates a *symbolic link*. The following example creates a symbolic link (i.e., cross-device link):

% **ln -s /usr/myfile /usr1/s_linkfile**

To verify that **linkfile** is really only a link and not an exact copy, we can use the **ls** command. In this case, we use the special option **-i**. This option shows the inode or index node number for the file. UNIX uses an *inode number*, or integer

number, that is unique for each file and directory for a given file system. Only hard links can use the same inode number. The following example shows the results after a link has been created:

    % ls -l myfile hard_linkfile
    151909 -rw-r--r--   2 rodney   24 Aug 25 17:05 hard_linkfile
    151909 -rw-r--r--   2 rodney   24 Aug 25 17:05 myfile

The number on the far left-hand side of the results shows that both files utilize the same inode number (i.e., 151909). Therefore, **hard_linkfile** is only a link to **myfile**. Now let us see if the inode numbers are the same for a symbolically linked file:

    % ls -li myfile linkfile
    151919 lrwxrwxrwx   1 rodney   6 Aug 25 17:08 s_linkfile -> myfile
    151909 -rw-r--r--   1 rodney   4 Aug 25 17:05 myfile

Notice in this case that the inode numbers are different; however, **s_linkfile** shows that it is really a pointer to the file **myfile** (file permissions start with a 1). Therefore, when you attempt to open and read the file **s_linkfile**, you really open and read the file **myfile**. Again, symbolic links are special because they allow the user to link files across UNIX file systems. This is important, especially when you are using UNIX networking software such as the Network File System (NFS) from Sun. NFS allows users to use remote disk devices over the ethernet as if they are local devices. Linking across remote or local file systems is only possible using symbolic links.

It is important to note that a link is really just a reference or pointer to the original file. The same rules regarding permissions for regular files apply to link files as well. For example, if the file **myfile** has read, write, and execute permissions, the user can display, modify, or execute the program using either the link file or the source file (**myfile**). The user can also change the permissions on the file **hard_linkfile** because they created the link. However, if the destination file **myfile** does not provide read and write permissions, the user will not be able to display or edit the contents of **s_linkfile** or **hard_linkfile**. The file **s_linkfile** can be removed; however, the contents of the data blocks referenced by **s_linkfile** cannot be read, modified/deleted, or executed. The following example shows that only the root user can read, write, or execute the file **myfile**. Any user other than the root user will receive errors when attempting to read/display, edit, or execute the link file **s_linkfile**:

```
% ls -l myfile
-rwx------  1 root        0 Apr  3 17:11 myfile
% ln -s myfile s_linkfile
% cat s_linkfile
cat: s_linkfile: Permission denied
% ed s_linkfile
?s_linkfile: Permission denied
q
% s_linkfile
s_linkfile: Permission denied.
```

Exercise 3

1 What command creates a hard link between two files?

2 What command verifies that the inode numbers are identical?

3 Remove the link and create a symbolic link from the file to another file system. You can use the **df** command to show the amount of free disk space available for each mounted file system. Alternatively, you can use the **mount** command to see all mounted file systems. You may need your system administrator's help to create a source or link file on another file system (you must have write permission to the other directory). A better approach may be to create a link from the other file system to your local directory. In the following example, we create a link **mylink** in our local directory that is a pointer to the file **foobar** located in the **/usr1** file system:

4 % **ln /usr1/foobar/file mylink**

chapter 4

The Shell, Redirection, Pipes, and Metacharacters

*T*he UNIX shell provides a command-line interface to the operating system, as was discussed in Chapter 1. The shell is also called a command-line interpreter, because it reads each user command and searches for the requested file for execution. The carriage return tells the shell that you have finished the construction of one command and are ready for the system to process your request (command). When the shell has completed processing of your current command, a prompt is provided to start the process all over. The UNIX system, in the past, has typically provided two command interfaces, the Bourne shell and the C shell. The Bourne shell has provided the basis for the C shell as well as the Korn shell (ksh). Therefore, our discussion starts with the Bourne shell, or **sh**. The following commands and features are discussed in this chapter:

- The Bourne shell
- Environment variables
- Other Bourne shell environment variables
- Redirection and appending output data

- Redirection and input data
- Pipes
- Background jobs
- Metacharacters
- Advanced metacharacters
- Metacharacter examples using **grep, egrep,** and **tr**

4.1 THE BOURNE SHELL

The Bourne shell, written by Steven Bourne, was the original shell provided with the UNIX operating system. If you are not running the Bourne shell, you need to type **sh** to start a Bourne shell. The prompt should become a dollar sign by default.

The shell provides the ability to construct commands with arguments or special command options. Each argument or option must be separated by a space or tab, which is also known as an internal field separator (IFS). The IFS allows the shell to interpret or parse the special requirements you have for a given command. For example, in earlier chapters, we used options for the **ls** command to see a long listing with the -l option or the file's inode number with a -i. These options are usually preceded by a minus, "-", to tell the command interpreter that we are now providing an option, not a file name (see **getopts** for further details). After all, there is nothing wrong with having a file called l or i (even though that does not tell you very much about the purpose of the file and should be discouraged). If the following command line were provided to the **ls** command, it would expect to find and list a file called l and i, because we did not precede each letter (option) with a minus:

    $ ls l i
    i not found
    l not found

The shell comes with a set of built-in functions. These built-in functions are included in the Bourne shell **/bin/sh** and are not contained in a separate file like the **ls** command. One of the many functions provided by the shell is special handling of signals. A signal in UNIX is much like a traffic signal. When the light is red, you better stop or risk having an accident. The same is true for UNIX signals (you can also have data and program crashes). For example, if you want to abort or **kill** a command after it has started, you can usually use the control and C keys together. This is like sending a red light to the program via the UNIX kernel, because the kernel is really in the driver's seat after you enter a command. UNIX has many signals that are defined by the **stty** command. Using the **stty**

command without any arguments provides the following default results on a Sun 4.1.3—based system:

```
$ stty -a
speed 9600 baud, 24 rows, 80 columns
-parenb -parodd cs8 -cstopb -hupcl cread -clocal -crtscts
-ignbrk brkint ignpar -parmrk -inpck -istrip -inlcr -igncr icrnl -iuclc
ixon -ixany -ixoff imaxbel
isig iexten icanon -xcase echo echoe echok -echonl -noflsh -tostop
echoctl -echoprt echoke
opost -olcuc onlcr -ocrnl -onocr -onlret -ofill -ofdel
erase kill  werase rprnt  flush lnext susp  intr  quit  stop  eof
^?   ^U   ^W   ^R   ^O   ^V   ^Z/^Y ^C   ^\   ^S/^Q ^D
```

The complete output just provided requires the **-a** flag for BSD systems and **-everything** for System V systems. Two of the more interesting **stty** local mode settings are for the end of file, **eof**, and interrupt, or **intr**. The EOF (control D) is used to terminate input from the keyboard. For example, when we are using the **cat** command to redirect input from the keyboard to a disk file, we need to use the control and D keys together to terminate input. The **intr** local **tty** mode (control and C keys used together) is used to interrupt processing of a command. For example, if we want to stop a command in the middle of execution, use the control and C keys together.

Exercise 1

1 What command allows you to view your current terminal settings?

2 What command changes your default settings for the **erase** function so that you can correct input from the command line with a control H (backspace key)?

4.2 ENVIRONMENT VARIABLES

One of the most important environment variables in the UNIX shell is the **PATH** variable. This variable is important because it is used to identify what directories are searched whenever an attempt is made to execute a command. For example, when we execute the command **ls** or **cp**, the shell must determine where to go and find the file **ls** or **cp** and execute the file as a program. It is easy to display the contents of the **PATH** environment variable using the **echo** command, as follows (you can also use the **set** command to display variable settings):

> $ **echo $PATH**
> /usr/bin:/bin:/usr/lib

In the preceding example, the shell first searches for executable programs in the **/usr/bin** directory. Next, the **/bin** directory is searched and finally the **/usr/lib** directory is used. If my command request (file to execute) cannot be located in any of these directories provided by the **PATH**, the following happens:

> $ **non_existing_file**
> non_existing_file: Command not found.

If, on the other hand, we provided a valid file name for execution to the shell prompt, the shell would locate the file from the search path and go to the appropriate directory and execute the file automatically. The **which** command is useful because it shows where a file is located in our current **PATH** environment variable. The following example shows where the shell first finds the **ls** command:

> $ **which ls**
> /bin/ls

It is important to note that if we had multiple versions of the **ls** program, the first occurrence that is located in our search **PATH**, starting from **/usr/bin** and ending with **/usr/lib**, will be used. If we created a different version of **ls** in the **/usr/bin** directory, the shell would use that version first. Therefore, it is always important to know the location for a command that you are going to execute, especially if someone is trying play a joke, for example, if someone creates an evil version of the **ls** program and copies it to your home directory. Now, when you type **cd** to go to the home directory and enter **ls**, the local **ls** program will **echo** the following message:

WARNING ALL YOUR FILES WILL BE REMOVED NOW!

We can always change our **PATH** to avoid these problems. To change the **PATH** from the shell prompt, you can add (append/preappend) or create a completely new **PATH** (remove). (There is no easy way to remove directories from your existing **PATH** without specifying a completely new **PATH**.) The following example appends the **/tmp** directory to our existing **PATH** (identified by **$PATH**, which is the contents of the variable):

```
$ PATH=$PATH:/tmp
$ export PATH
```

The **export** command is important, because it makes our **PATH** globally available to all child processes or shells. Directories also can be placed before the current **PATH** setting. It is important to note that the colon is an important delimiter for separation of directories. The following example places the **/usr/tmp** directory as the first directory in our search **PATH** followed by our current settings (i.e., contents of $PATH):

```
$ PATH=/usr/tmp:$PATH
$ export PATH
```

The export command is really not needed in the second example, because it was already used in the previous example. However, if we were to exit the current shell, the **PATH** assignment and **export** commands would be lost.

Therefore, one more important point needs to be made about the **PATH** environment variable. It is always best to set your **PATH** in the **.profile** file located in your home directory. This file is read by the shell every time you log in to the UNIX system. Just changing the PATH environment variable from the shell is only effective for your current process and all child processes (if you use the **export** command). You can create a child process by entering the command **sh.** This creates another Bourne shell that becomes a child of the previous (parent) shell. Your commands now are provided to the child shell. To return to the previous parent shell, simply type **exit.**

Exercise 2

1 What command allows you to start a Bourne shell?

2 What commands allow you to review the current settings for your **PATH** environment variable?

3 What command appends the directory **/tmp** to your current PATH?

4 What command makes this new PATH available to all child shell processes?

Exercise 2 (Continued)

5 Create an executable file called **myfile** that is a shell script that contains the **date** command. Move the program to the **/tmp** directory. What command allows you to see where (which directory) the shell finds the command **myfile**?

6 Now change directories to some location other than **/tmp** and execute the program **myfile**.

7 Did the shell find and execute your program?

4.3 OTHER BOURNE SHELL ENVIRONMENT VARIABLES

To see the rest of the environment variables available with the Bourne shell, use the **set** command, as follows:

```
$ set
PS1=$
PS2=>
TERM=xterm
HOME=/mnt/rodney
PATH=/usr/bin:/bin:/usr/lib:/tmp
```

There are many other variables as well. The **PS1** and **PS2** variables define the primary and secondary prompt settings respectively. In the preceding case, our primary prompt is the dollar sign because we are running the UNIX Bourne shell. The **PS2** variable is a secondary prompt for when we have to continue command-line input to an additional line. This can be accomplished using the back-slash character, "\", as follows:

```
$ The_ other_ approach_ is_ to_ use_ the_ \
>character_ to_ continue_ input
```

Because we used the "\" character for line continuation, the secondary prompt ">" appears on the second line. We can change **PS1** or **PS2** using the same syntax that was used for the PATH environment variable, as follows:

```
$ PS2="secondary_prompt "
```

In this case, the double-quote characters are used because we want a space after our secondary prompt to help distinguish between input characters and the prompt itself. The **TERM** variable shows the type of display device we are using. Because we are using the X Window System, our terminal type is set to **xterm**. Our **HOME** environment variable is set (by default) during the log in process by the shell after it reads the contents of **/etc/passwd**.

The following example shows how to set the primary prompt to the system host name instead of our log in name. The double quotes are used to add a space at the end of the host name and allow us to distinguish our input from the shell prompt:

> \$ PS1="'hostname' > "
> jupiter> echo \$PS1
> jupiter>

Exercise 3

1 Change your secondary prompt environment variable to display your log in name. (*Hint*: Use the **whoami** command to obtain your current log in name.)

2 What command changes your secondary prompt to the string "second prompt> "?

4.4   REDIRECTION AND APPENDING OUTPUT DATA

Redirection, as you will recall, is useful for sending the output of a command to a file, not to the display device. However, one problem with redirection is that you may also want to preserve the existing contents of the file and simply append data to the end. By using the double greater-than sign, the output is appended:

> \$ cat >> existing_file
> I am going to append this data
> to the end of the file called
> existing_file. When I am done, I still
> need to use the control and D keys together
> to send an end of file signal like so.
> ^D

To verify that the contents of **existing_file** have been preserved and the new data have only been appended to the end, use the **cat** command:

$ cat existing_file
This line already existed in the file
So did this file
This was the last line in the original file
I am going to append this data
to the end of the file called
existing_file. When I am done, I still
need to use the control and D keys together
to send an end of file signal like so.

Exercise 4

1 Use output file redirection to place the results of the **ls** command in a file called **lsfile**.

2 Now append to **lsfile** the results of executing the **date** command. Make sure to preserve the results of **lsfile** when you write the date and time information.

3 What happens if you attempt to redirect output to a file when you do not have write permission?

4.5 REDIRECTION AND INPUT DATA

Reading input from a file using redirection is the opposite of output redirection. Instead of writing data from a command to an output file, data are read from the file and used as input. The following command example opens the file **inputfile** and sends the data as input to the **sort** command:

$ sort < inputfile

This is actually a silly way of performing a sort on the data contained in the file **inputfile**. We can accomplish the same task without using the input redirection symbol. However, the following **mail** example is much more useful. In this case, we open the contents of the file **status_report** and send it as a mail message to the user boss:

$ mail boss < status_report

It is mandatory to include the user name before specifying the input redirection symbol (when using the **mail** command). The redirection symbol must be followed by a valid file name that contains the message we want to send. In this case, the shell opens the file **status_report** and reads these data until it reaches the end of file. It is also a good idea to include the -s option followed by a subject name, because the **mail** program no longer prompts for a subject.

Exercise 5

1 Use the input redirection operator and send yourself a copy of the file **/etc/group**.

2 Verify that you were able to perform this operation successfully by reading your mail.

3 Now include subject information in your mail message and send youself a copy of the **/etc/motd** file.

4.6 PIPES

One of the most powerful tools available with the UNIX shell is the pipe facility, " | ". A *pipe* provides the ability to take output from one command and provide it as input to another command. Pipes are different from redirection, because they deal with command-to-command interfaces (pipe lines). Redirection, on the other hand, only takes the output of a command and provides the results as input to a file (not a command, as is the case with a pipe). A simple example of the pipe command is to join the **ls** command and the **sort** command together for special data processing. For example, to **sort** the results of the **ls** output, execute the following command:

```
$ ls | sort
1994.rod
1994.rod.backup
performance.help
performance.review
```

You can continue to join commands together using pipes to accomplish many tasks. For example, to print the results of the preceding command on the line printer, we could add the following to the previous command:

$ ls | sort | lpr

One problem with pipes is that we are no longer able to see the results of the command execution. The preceding command prints the results of listing our current working directory in sorted order; however, we are not able to see any output data on our display. The **tee** command helps solve the problem of blocking output. The **tee** command allows the user to both send the output of a command as input to another command and see the output results on the display device. The following example sends sorted data from **ls** to the line printer, but we are also able to review the results on our display (**/dev/tty**):

$ ls | sort | tee /dev/tty | lpr

Exercise 6

1 Print the sorted results on the display as well as the line printer from a long and recursive listing of your current working directory.

2 Add to the command a filter that only prints files that start with the letters "a" through "p".

4.7 BACKGROUND JOBS

Because UNIX is a multitasking operating system, the ability to execute a program in the background is provided by the shell. Background processing prevents the user from waiting for one program to complete execution before starting the next. In other words, the user can start one program (e.g., **mail**) and either suspend or put it in the background while starting another program (e.g., **lpr** or **lp**). The "&" character is used to start a program in the background. If you are using the C or Korn shell, you can use the control and Z keys together to interrupt and suspend a program that is currently running in the foreground. The **jobs** command (C and Korn shells only) displays all background jobs and is useful for identifying the job number of a suspended program. The **bg** command (C and Korn shells only) followed by the job number id continues running the program in the

background. You can terminate a program that is suspended or running in the background using the **kill** command (C and Korn shells only) followed by the job number. Use the Bourne shell if you want to copy a large file but not wait for the copy operation to complete; type the following:

   $ cp bigfile /tmp/ &

Notice that the "&" symbol is located at the end of the line. Therefore, when a command is submitted that may never complete, the shell prompt is returned immediately. In the preceding example, even though the copy command may take a long time to complete, the shell prompt returns immediately, because the command is processed in the background. In the preceding example, there is no need to specify the file name after the **/tmp** directory. However, if I wanted to call the file something other than **bigfile**, that name must be specified. For example, to copy **bigfile** to **/tmp** with a new name of **newbigfile**, execute the following:

   $ cp bigfile /tmp/newbigfile

Another command that is useful for verification of a file is the **sum** command. This command calculates a checksum and displays the file size in kilobytes. Enter the command **sum** followed by the first file name and record the results.

Exercise 7

1 Copy a big file to your home directory in the background (**/etc/termcap** is one possibility).

2 Verify that your copy operation was successful using the **diff** command.

3 What other command can be used to compare two files?

4 Start editing a file using **vi**, **ex**, or **ed**. In the middle of your editing, you suddenly remember that you need to send an important mail message to a friend about lunch. Suspend your edits and invite yourself to lunch with an important mail message. Finally, return to your edit session.

To see processes running in the background, use the **ps** command (process status). If you identify a process running in the background that you want to terminate, use the **kill** command with the process id (PID). The C shell's **kill** command accepts either a process id or job number from the **jobs** command. The Bourne shell only accepts a process id number as follows:

```
$ cat > foobar &
$ ps
 PID TT STAT TIME COMMAND
18247 p5 S 0:04 -sh (csh)
22995 p5 T 0:00 cat
22996 p5 R 0:00 ps
$ kill 22995
$ ps
 PID TT STAT TIME COMMAND
18247 p5 S 0:04 -sh (csh)
22996 p5 R 0:00 ps
```

4.8 METACHARACTERS

One of the more powerful features of the UNIX shell is the use of metacharacters. Many of these special characters were mentioned in previous chapters. For review, the "*" metacharacter will match any number of occurrences of any character, where the "?" metacharacter only matches one occurrence of any character. Other useful metacharaters are square brackets, "[" and "]". The brackets are useful for identifying a list or range of characters. For example, assume that you wanted to list files that only started with the letters, "a" to "p". The following command satisfies these requirements:

```
$ ls [a-p]*
```

Exercise 8

1 Use the **ls** command to list all matching files in your current working directory that start with the letters b through j.

2 List all files in your directory that have only a one character file name from w to p.

3 List files that only end in the letters l to p.

4 List all files from b to j and l to p.

4.9   ADVANCED METACHARACTERS

The following metacharacters are also provided by the shell and useful for searching and sorting. Practice using these functions using the **grep** and **egrep** commands. For further help with these metacharacters, see the examples provided in the next section. Here is the contents of the data file:

> **$ cat datafile**
> First
> First Last
> Last First

The caret, "^", is used for matching a string at the beginning of a line. For example, to match all the lines in all the files in the current working directory that start with the string "First", use the following command:

> **$ grep \^First datafile**
> First
> First Last

The dollar sign, $, is used to match strings that occur at the end of a line. The following command matches the string starting with "Last" at the end of a line:

> **$ grep 'Last$' datafile**
> First Last

Notice that I now used the single-quote character instead of the back slash. I could have performed the same task using the following:

> **$ grep Last\$ datafile**

The period matches any single character and .* matches any number of characters. For example, to find all strings starting with the letter L followed by any two characters and then the letter t (Last, List, etc.), use the following:

> **$ grep 'L..t' datafile**
> First Last
> Last First

The asterisk is used to match zero or more characters, for example, a string starting with F followed by any number of characters and then ending with the letter t (the asterisk must be escaped from the shell, so single quotes are used):

    $ grep 'F.*t' datafile
    First
    First Last
    Last First

4.10 METACHARACTER EXAMPLES USING GREP, EGREP, AND TR

The following example summarizes various options available for searching with the **grep** and **egrep** (extended **grep**) commands:

$ grep 'Your Name' file	Lines with "Your Name"
$ grep '\<Student\>' file	Lines with "Student"
$ grep '[A-P]' file	Lines with A to P characters
$ grep '^Beginning' file	Lines that begin with "Beginning"
$ grep 'ending$' file	Lines that end with "ending"
$ grep -v 'Name' file	Lines that do not contain "Name"
$ grep '$LITERAL' file	Lines that contain "$LITERAL"
$ grep '[a-cp-z]' *	Lines in all files from a to c and p to z
$ grep '^\<I>' file	Lines that start with the word I
$ grep '\<end\>$' file	Lines that end with the end
$ grep '^[a-b]...[1-3]' file	Lines that start with four characters with the letter a or b and end in a number 1 to 3
$ egrep '(Joe | Bill)' file	Lines that contain Joe or Bill
$ egrep '^ +' *	Lines in all files that start with one or more spaces
$ egrep '^ *' *	Lines in all files that start with zero or more spaces

The **tr** command is used to translate characters. Square brackets are very useful for translating a range of characters from one class to another. For example, the following command translates all uppercase characters to lowercase[*]:

    $ tr '[A-Z]' '[a-z]' < oldfile > newfile

Notice we used the input redirection symbol (less than) to open the file **oldfile** to read in the data. The file **newfile** was used to write our output results after translation from uppercase to lowercase. We could have also used the pipe symbol and the **tee** command to write the results to both the screen as well as the output file **newfile**.

Exercise 9

1 Copy the **/etc/passwd** file to your current working directory and call the copy **mypasswd.**

2 What command searches for the string "root" at the start of each line in the **mypasswd** file?

3 What command searches for the string "sh" at the end of each line in the **mypasswd** file?

4 What command checks for words that start with the letters A through F for all files contained in the current working directory?

5 What command displays all lines that start with your log in name in the file **mypasswd**?

6 Translate all lowercase letters from p to z to uppercase letters in the file **mypasswd.**

---

*UNIX is case-sensitive to uppercase r and lowercase letters. The file **CAT** is not the same as **cat.** However, if you log in to UNIX in uppercase, it will remap all commands to uppercase. If this happens, it is suggested that you exit the shell and use the control and D keys together after turning off caps lock. This creates a new **login** session in lowercase.

chapter **5** ▶

The ex and vi Editors and the ksh (Korn Shell)

*T*his chapter discusses three of the more common editors available with the UNIX operating system. It starts with the most basic editor, **ed**. This is followed by a more advanced version of **ed** called **ex**. Finally, we move from the **ed** and **ex** line-oriented editors to the visual or screen editor, **vi**.

5.1   THE EX EDITOR

Remember, we used the following commands in Chapter 1 to create a new file using the **ex** editor that contained three lines of text:

% **ed newfile**
a

> This is new text for which I am creating the file.
> I will need to enter a period "." on a line by itself to
> terminate input.
> .
> **1,$p**
> This is new text for which I am creating the file.
> I will need to enter a period "." on a line by itself to
> terminate input.
> **w**
> **q**

We also said that lines could be deleted using the **d** command inside the **ed** editor. However, we did not forget to mention the **u** command for undo. The **u** command allows you to undo the last command, in this case, a delete operation. One of the many nice features provided with the **ex** editor is the ability to specify multiple files for editing. After we have completed changes, followed by a write command, the next file can be edited by using the **n** command, as follows:

> **% ed file1 file2**
> "file1" 1 line, 9 characters
> **:q**
> 1more file to edit
> **:n**
> "file2" No such file or directory
> **:q**

In this case, **file1** and **file2** are both new files. When a **q** command was typed, while editing **file1**, **ex** wanted to make sure that I was aware that there was still one more file ready for editing (i.e., **file2**). When command **n** was provided, the **ex** editor automatically opened **file2** for editing (a new file that did not exist).

The **ex** editor also provides the ability to change to visual mode using the **vi** editor. (Just type **vi** at the **ex** command prompt.) When you want to return to **ex** from **vi**, use the control and \ keys together. We are going to discuss the **vi** editor next.

Another useful feature in the **ex** editor (also available with the **vi** editor) is the ability to join lines. To join line 2 with line 1, simply type a **j** while positioned on line number 1, as follows:

> **% ex myfile**
> "myfile" 4 lines, 24 characters
> **:1,$p**

```
Mary and Joe need to complete the
test plan and schedule by June
in order to make the beta ship date of
June 1994.
:1
Mary and Joe need to complete the
:j
Mary and Joe need to complete the test plan and schedule by June
:1,$p
Mary and Joe need to complete the test plan and schedule by June
in order to make the beta ship date of
June 1994.
:q
No write since last change (:quit! overrides)
:q!
```

In this example, we first print the contents of the file **myfile** (**1,$p**). Next, we position to line number 1. Now we can join line number 2 with line 1. We then print the contents of the file again to verify the join operation was successful. Finally, we attempt to quit; however, because we have modified the original contents of **myfile**, we receive a warning message that we should use the command **q!** to override our changes (do not save changes, just quit). In order to leave the **ex** editor, you must either use the **w** and **q** commands together to save your changes or **q!** (as I did) to ignore any changes and simply quit. The **q!** command leaves the file contents intact (no change from when the editor was first entered).

You can also position your current line position up using the - key, or down using the + or carriage return keys. If you are brave, you can also test the recovery option **-r** of the **ex** editor. This option is most useful when the system crashes while you are in the middle of editing a file. After the system restarts, type **ex -r** followed by the name of the file you were editing. We hope your changes will have been preserved in a temporary file (located in **/tmp**), so you can recover all changes prior to the crash. Something similar to the following **mail** message should be sent to you by the system if a recovery file is available after the reboot process has completed:

```
Date: Wed, 31 Aug 94 18:42:05 -0700
From: root (Operator - Rodney Wilson)
Message-Id: <9409010142.AA00135@rodney>
Subject: editor saved "/tmp/Re27402"
Apparently-To: rodney
Status: R
```

You were editing the file "/tmp/Re27402"
at <Wed Aug 31 15:35> on the machine "rodney"
when the system went down.

You can retrieve most of your changes to this file
using the "recover" command of the editor.
An easy way to do this is to give the command "vi -r /tmp/Re27402".

Another useful feature of **ex** is the ability to yank and put text within a file. A yank operation is really the same as a copy operation. The yank (**ya**) command allows the user to copy a line or several lines of text and store the data in a temporary buffer. Next, the user can position to a new line location and use the put (**pu**) command to place the text from the copy buffer in the new location. The following example yanks the text "My status report" and puts a copy of the text on the last line of the file **status_report**:

```
% ex status_report
"status_report" 3 lines, 80 characters
:1,$p
My status report
This is my status report.
This is the end of my status report.
:1
My status report
:ya
:3
This is the end of my status report.
:pu
My status report
:1,$p
My status report
This is my status report.
This is the end of my status report.
My status report
:w
:q
```

Exercise 1

1 What commands allow you to copy and paste a line of text?

2 Test the ability to edit multiple files using the **ex** editor. What command provides this ability?

3 Verify that you can quit the editor without changing the text in your file. What command provides this ability?

4 What commands allow you to move up and down lines while editing a file?

5 What command should you use to attempt and recover your changes after a crash?

5.2 THE VI EDITOR

The **vi**, or visual, editor provides a superset of the functions provided by the **ex** and **ed** editors. One major benefit of **vi** is that it provides a full screen rather than a line-by-line method of editing. The most important thing to remember when first learning to use the **vi** editor is that there are two modes of operation. The first mode is the command mode. This mode is used for processing commands such as adding or deleting text and is the mode that you always enter when you first edit a file. The other mode in **vi** is the text mode. This mode is used for entering text or data in your file. The user must use the escape key followed by a command to return from the text mode back to command mode, for example, to reposition your cursor above or below the current cursor position (escape up, or down arrow). It is strongly suggested that new users use the following command after entering the **vi** editor to help identify what mode they are in (SVR4 systems only):

:set showmode

Now, if the user enters an **i** for the insert mode, the editor will display "INSERT MODE" in the lower right-hand corner of the display. If the user uses the command **o**, "OPEN MODE" will be shown in the lower right-hand corner of the display. The **a** command (append text) will be displayed as "APPEND MODE" in the same screen location.

The first thing you often notice when first creating a file with the **vi** editor is that your screen contains a series of lines that begin with the tilde ("~") character. Each line represents an unallocated or unused line of text. This means that the line really does not exist in the file; however, you can use the **o** or **a** command and continue to depress the carriage return to open or allocate new lines. Each carriage return then allocates a new line for you to use. At the same time (for each carriage return), you notice that the tilde character disappears.

You can use the escape key to return to the command mode and then use the **h** key for moving left, **j** for down, **k** for up, and **l** for right. Oftentimes, the arrow keys on your keyboard can also be used; however, you need to make sure that your **TERM** (Bourne shell) or **term** (C shell) environment variables are set to match the correct terminal or display you are currently using.

If you become stuck in **vi**, the best thing to remember is to always use the escape key followed by a **:q!** (quit without saving your changes). Otherwise, you can use the **:wq** command or **ZZ** to write and quit with your changes.

To insert text to the left of the text cursor, use the **i** command. Remember again, you must be in the command mode, which requires you to use the escape key first. Alternatively, you can use the **a** command to append text to the right of the text cursor. This is useful if you want to first position to the end of a line with the **$** command and enter an **a** for the append mode. If you would like to open a new line below your current position, simply use the **o** command. To open a line above your current position, use the **O** command.

Now that we have appended, inserted, and opened lines for adding text, let us discuss how to delete text. To delete a single character in the command mode, position to the text you want to delete and use the **x** key. Each time you use the **x** command, you delete the character to the right of your current cursor position (you must be in the command mode, so make sure to use the escape key). If you would like to delete a word, you can use the **dw** command. To delete the entire line, type **dd**. Finally, to delete from the current cursor position to the end of the line, type **d$**. Remember, the $ says the end of the line. You can also delete any number of lines below your current position by simply typing a **d** followed by the number of lines to delete and a carriage return. The **u** command also undoes your last delete.

Now give the **vi** editor a try.

Exercise 2

1 What commands in **vi** allow you to insert, append, and open text in the file? Which side of the cursor does the text go when you use the insert function? How about the append function?

2 What command allows you to position immediately to the end of a line?

3 What command allows you to move immediately to the beginning of a line?

4 What command shows you the mode you are currently in (i.e., insert, open, append)?

5 What commands deletes characters, words, and lines?

6 How can you delete from your current position to the end of the line?

Global Search and Replace

You can also use the **/** character, in the command mode, to search for a string in a file. Use the **N** command to search backward and **n** to return searching forward in the file. At the end of Chapter 4, there are several metacharacters and regular expressions that are useful for searching inside **vi**. It is often helpful to return to the **ex** editor from **vi** to perform complex functions. For example, to perform a global search and replace of the string "Student" with "Teacher", enter the following command inside **vi**:

:1,$s/Student/Teacher

One problem with this command is that it only replaces the first occurrence of the string Student with Teacher on each line. In order to replace every occurrence on every line, we need to add the global **g** command at the end, as follows:

1,$s/Student/Teacher/g

Exercise 3

1 What command searches forward in the file starting at the current line position for a specific string of text?

2 What command continues to search forward in the file for the same string?

3 How can you search backward in the file?

4 How do you begin a new search for a string starting at the current line position and work backward?

5 How can you globally change all occurrences of a particular string to a new value?

Reading Files and Command Output

Another benefit of dropping into the **ex** editor from **vi** is the ability to read in the contents of a file or results from executing a command. Use the **:r** command to drop into the **ex** editor and request the editor to read in the contents of a file. A space is needed between the **r** command and the file name to read from:

:r mynewfile

This causes the contents of the file **mynewfile** to be read into the current **vi** file at the current cursor location. Therefore, if you want the contents of the file to be placed at the end of the file, first use the **G** command from the command mode. Next, use the preceding command (**:r** to read a file and write the contents at the end of the file). As mentioned before, you can also read in the results of executing a command and store the output in the file at the current line position. The following example reads in the results of executing the **date** command and stores the date and time at the current cursor position in the file:

:r !date

Another useful example of this feature is the program to **mail** a binary file to another user. Use the **uuencode** command to prepare the file for mailing (the mail program only deals with text, not binary data). After entering the **vi** editor from **mail** using the **~v** command, use the following command to prepare the binary file **a.out** for the **mail** program:

:r !uuencode a.out a.out

The first occurrence of the string **a.out** is required to identify the name of the file to encode. The second occurrence of **a.out** is the name used as a file label (the name to which to write the data during the decode process). When users receive mail, now they can save the mail message as a file on the disk using the **s** command inside of **mail**. Next, they edit the file and strip out the mail header information. Finally, they must use the **uudecode** command followed by the edited mail file name to decode the file. This command results in making a binary executable file with the name **a.out**.

Exercise 4

1 What command can you use to read in the results of executing the **date** command after you have entered the **vi** editor? (You need to drop into the **ex** mode.)

2 How can you sort the output of the **ls** command and store the results after the results of the **date** command? (You perform this function while in **vi**.)

3 Now use **vi** to place comments by each file name for reference. This type of file is often called a README file in the UNIX world and is used to help document processes and products.

4 Finally, write the results of the **date** command, again at the end of the file while in **vi**.

Other Useful Commands

The **:w** command allows you to write the currently opened file to a new name and possibly directory location (if specified). This is especially useful after you have made several changes to a file and are now unable to write your changes to the file because of permission problems. By using the **:w** command followed by a new directory location and name, you are able to save your changes. After exiting **vi**, simply copy the file to the desired location (make sure to change the directory permissions using the **chmod** command in the directory where you need to make changes). The following example writes the current file with changes to the **/tmp** directory using the name **rodsfile**:

:w /tmp/rodsfile

Once this operation has completed, use the **:q!** command to quit without saving any changes. Another useful command is the "**~**". The tilde command allows you to change lowercase characters to uppercase and uppercase characters to lowercase. To change the case of a character, enter the command mode (depress the escape key) and depress the tilde key for each character you want to change.

Exercise 5

1 What command can you use to write the currently opened file to the **/tmp** directory with a file name called **yourname**?

2 What character allows you to change the case (uppercase to lowercase or lowercase to uppercase) of several words in the file before writing your file to a new location?

5.3 THE KSH

Once you have learned the **vi** editor, you will definitely want to take a look at the Korn shell (**ksh**). However, unless you have access to System V Release 4, or a well-supported system (e.g., Solaris, HP-UX, AIX, IRIX), you may not find the **ksh**. The **ksh** (pronounced kay-shell) provides a **vi** interface to previous **ksh** commands. To enable this facility, you must type the following to have the **ksh** use the **vi** open mode when an escape is entered at the command prompt. First, make sure you are running the **ksh** by typing the following:

    % ksh
    $ set -o vi

Notice that our prompt changed from the **csh** percent sign to a dollar sign. This is the default prompt for the **ksh**. Now change to the open mode and begin reviewing your history buffer by depressing the escape key. You are now in the command mode, just as if you were editing a text file in **vi**; however, the data you are editing are really previous **ksh** commands. The **h, j, k,** and **l** commands work as left, down, up, and right arrows, just as in the **vi** editor. To reexecute a command, position to the command using the arrow keys, or (**h, j, k,** and **l**) and enter a carriage return. If you want to change a command, use the same commands for modifying text in **vi**, as follows:

- **cw** to change a word
- **^** to position to the beginning of the current line
- **$** to position to the end of the current line
- **d$** to delete everything to the right of the cursor
- **i** to insert text to the left of the cursor
- **a** to append text to the right of the cursor
- **/string to** search forward in your history buffer for "string"
- **N** or **n** to search backward or forward for the current search string

---

Exercise 6

1 What command allows you to start the Korn shell?

2 How can you tell the Korn shell to edit your history buffer using the **vi** editor?

3 How can you modify previous commands by substituting, inserting, appending, and deleting previous parts of a command?

4 Spend some time with the **ksh**. It is a great way of getting to know the **vi** editor better!

chapter 6

The Bourne Shell

*T*his chapter provides several useful examples and exercises for the Bourne shell, or **sh**. As was mentioned earlier, the Bourne shell is a command interpreter for the UNIX system. This means that the shell parses user commands and instructions that are contained within a single command line and processes each request based on the new line and/or semicolon characters. A semicolon character allows the user to specify several commands on a single line, just as if several carriage returns were included between each command string.

The Bourne shell, as you will shortly see, provides many powerful features. However, you will also notice that several useful commands, such as repeating previous commands, are missing. However, most of the functions that are desired, and not provided by the Bourne shell, are usually provided by the C shell or Korn shell. These shells are discussed in the following chapters. It is good to start with the Bourne shell before continuing on to the more advanced shells, because the Bourne shell is the foundation for other shells. Many programmers still use the Bourne shell to write shell programs. Shell programs that contain many shell commands are also called shell scripts. The following features of the Bourne shell are provided in this chapter:

- Command subgrouping using **tar**
- Output and error redirection
- The grave accents
- Bourne shell programming basics
- Looping commands (**for** and **while**)
- Setting and unsetting variables
- Variable substitution
- The **expr** command
- The **case** statement
- The **shift** command
- Functions
- Trap handlers

6.1 COMMAND SUBGROUPING USING TAR

Because UNIX is a multiuser and multitasking operating system, several important events occur each time you enter a command. Each time a command is entered, a new process is created. This new process is called a child process of your current shell. UNIX uses a special kernel function called **fork** to create child processes. Each child process inherits the same permissions and ownership as the parent. Therefore, the child can create, read, write, and delete files in the same manner as the parent shell. In some cases, it is more desirable to have a single child process perform many commands. The shell requires the use of parentheses to identify a series of commands to be performed by a single child process. One of the best examples for when and why you would want to use *command subgroups*, or parentheses, can be shown using the **tar** command. The **tar** command provides the ability to copy files from one directory hierarchy to another. Therefore, the following command copies all the files in the **/usr/lib** directory and below to the **/tmp** directory:

$ **cd /usr/lib; tar cf - . | (cd /tmp; tar xf - .)**

Let us take a moment to discuss the preceding example in detail. First, we change directories to the source location for the copy using the **cd** command. Next, we use the semicolon to act as a delimiter for the start of the next command. The **tar** command says that we want to create a **tar** archive; however, the file is specified as the standard output device using the minus, "-", character. We also tell **tar** that we want to copy all files in the current directory and all subdirectories by specifying the period to represent the current working directory. This becomes the input data for the pipe (i.e., the next command). Next, we specify an open parenthesis to state that we want all the following commands to be performed by the

same child process (command subgroup). The first operation inside the parentheses is to change directories to **/tmp**. Next, we execute the **tar** command to start reading data from the pipe as input and extracting all data from the pipe (the first **tar** command). This is an ideal command example for command subgrouping, because the extraction of the data over a pipe must be performed in the new directory location (**/tmp**) by the same process. If we did not specify the change directory and **tar** extract commands to be performed by the same process, the data would not be extracted in the directory that we required (i.e., **/tmp**); it would be extracted back in the **/usr/lib** directory.

Exercise 1

1 Provide the appropriate command options to **tar** files from the **/tmp** directory to your home directory. (If you are not sure where your home directory is located, use the **cd** command by itself to change directories to your home directory.) Next, use the **pwd** command to print the current working directory (now your home directory).

2 Why is command subgrouping so important in this instance?

3 What happens if you do not use command subgrouping?

6.2   OUTPUT AND ERROR REDIRECTION

It is often useful to send output and error data from a command or shell script to a file. This file can then be used to help debug or diagnose any problems that may occur during program execution. For example, during installation of UNIX System V Release 4, each time a product or package is installed, a **mail** message is sent to the system administrator. If the package had a failure, the administrator will be able to read **mail** and determine the best way to correct the problem. However, without preserving or redirecting status, error, and output information, it is very difficult to determine how to correct the problem. As an example, the following program sends all error messages to the file called **errors** during execution of the **ls** command:

$ **ls 2> errors**

Normally, there should not be any data in the file called **errors**, because the **ls** command should work correctly, that is, unless the user does not have permission to read data in the current working directory (for example). The following example attempts to list a file called **foobarjar** in the current working directory. In this case the error message is stored in the file **errors**, as expected:

$ ls foobarjar 2> errors

Notice that the error message is not displayed on the screen because we told the shell to *redirect,* or send, all error information directly to the file **errors**. You can verify the contents of the file **errors** using the **cat** command, as follows:

$ cat errors
foobarjar not found

Because the standard error file descriptor is 2 and the standard input is 0, file descriptor 1 must be used for output. The following example outputs a list of the current files and directories to a file called **listfile**:

$ ls 1> listfile

This command is the same as output redirection to a file:

$ ls > listfile

The next command redirects error messages (file descriptor 2) to the same file as specified for output redirection (file descriptor 1). In other words, error messages should be redirected to the same place as output.

$ ls > listfile 2>&1

Exercise 2

1　Use the output redirection symbol to redirect output from the **ls** command to a file in the **/tmp** directory (use any file name).

2　Enter a command name that you do not believe the shell will be able to find (e.g., **sjfjkldsjfk**) and send the error message from the shell to a file called **myerrors** located in the **/tmp** directory.

3　Enter another bad (i.e., nonexistent) file name and append the error data to the file **myerrors**. Verify that the file contains the error message.

6.3   THE GRAVE ACCENTS (BACK QUOTES)

Use the grave accents to store results of command execution as a string for variable assignment. In other words, you can execute a command and provide the output as a string literal or constant value. This output can be displayed using the **echo** command or assigned to a variable (in the C shell, the **set** command must be used):

> $ **echo 'date'**
> Mon Aug 29 15:55:04 PDT 1994
> $ **date_variable='date'**

Note that the grave accents did not display the string "date" as is provided by the following three commands, but it actually provided the results of executing the **date** command as input using the **echo** command:

> $ **echo 'date' ; echo date; echo "date"**
> date
> date
> date

The next example uses the grave accents to assign the current date and time to the variable **date_variable** that then can be displayed using the **echo** command:

> $ **date_variable='date'**
> $ **echo $date_variable**
> Mon Aug 29 15:59:49 PDT 1994

The following example assigns the variable **total** the addition of two variables ($a and $b) using the **expr** command:

> $ **total='expr $a + $b'**
> $ **echo "a = "$a; echo "b = "$b; echo "total = "$total**
> a = 5
> b = 3
> total = 8

Exercise 3

1 What special characters can be used to **echo** the results of executing a command (e.g., **date**) as a string literal? How can you display "The date is" on your screen followed by the results of executing the date command?

2 Try to construct a single command to **echo** the value of a string literal (i.e., "My name is") and the results of executing the **whoami** command all on the same line.

6.4 BOURNE SHELL PROGRAMMING BASICS

The Bourne shell provides a basic set of tools that can be very useful for programmers to perform many tasks. Earlier, we defined a *shell script* as a file that contains a set of commands that can be used to perform many functions. Shell scripts can also contain *conditional statements*. A conditional statement allows a branch in control flow (program execution) to occur when a certain state or condition is true or false. For example, the following condition displays "everything is fine" when the previous command is completed successfully. Otherwise, the conditional (**if**) will say that "everything is NOT fine". Also, note that the Bourne shell has a built-in variable "$?" that holds the return status for every command. When command execution is successful, the return status is usually set to zero; otherwise, a failure has occurred. The following example checks if the **date** command is successful:

```
$ date
Mon Aug 29 15:59:49 PDT 1994
$ if test "$?" = "0"
> then
>       echo "everything is fine"
> else
>       echo "everything is NOT fine"
> fi
everything is fine
```

Notice that the shell immediately provides the secondary prompt defined by the **PS2** environment variable after the first line of the **if** statement. This is

because the shell treats the **if** statement as a compound statement that requires the line continuation prompt provided by the **PS2** prompt. The **test** command provides many options for evaluating the results of an expression. If the expression is true, the **test** command will provide a result of 0. If the expression is false, the **test** command will provide a nonzero value. Most UNIX commands provide a zero on success and nonzero on failure. This value is stored or returned in the special built-in variable $? after the command completes execution. It is generally good programming practice to include tabs for each **if** condition statement when nesting occurs and for each **then** and **else** statement as follows:

```
if test "$?" = "0"
then
        echo "everything is fine"
else
        echo "everything is NOT fine"
fi
```

Exercise 4

1 Create a shell script using the **vi** editor to display "success" or "failure" depending on if the name the user enters matches the log in name correctly. The shell script must correctly determine the user's real log in name as a value contained in a variable (derived from a UNIX command). Remember, a good tester always tests both success and failure conditions.

6.5   LOOPING COMMANDS (THE FOR COMMAND)

The **for** command provides the ability to loop through a series of words or strings contained in a "word list". This command steps through each item in the name list and assigns each value to a variable. The following example steps through each file in the current working directory and assigns each name to a variable called **file**. The contents of the variable **file** are displayed each time through the loop; however, we could perform a much more useful operation such as searching for a string or editing the file with the **vi** editor if we desired:

```
$ for file in `ls`
> do
```

```
>      echo $file
> done
a
b
c
```

Notice that the secondary prompt is provided after the first **for** statement (just as was the case with the **if** statement). It is important to point out that the output of **ls** is what is provided as a word list to the **for** command. Also, we are displaying the contents of the variable **$file**, not the variable name itself (the dollar sign in front of a name tells the shell we want the value of a variable, not the variable itself).

Exercise 5

1 Create a shell script that loops through a list of files to edit in the current working directory. Make sure that each file name starts with the letters a to q and w to z.

2 Copy your program and modify it so that it prompts users if they want to remove the file in the list, each time through the loop. (*Hint*: Use the **-i** option of the **rm** command.)

6.6 LOOPING COMMANDS (THE WHILE COMMAND)

The **while** command is a looping command that can be used to continue looping until a state change. As an example, to loop forever, we can use the following:

```
$ while true
> do
> echo "To be or not to be...."
> done
To be or not to be....
To be or not to be....
To be or not to be....
To be or not to be....
^C
```

Because the condition **true** always is true, this loop never terminates.

However, if the user interrupts the preceding script with the control and C keys together, the loop will terminate. Another, example of looping is to include an input value check in the body of a loop and continue to loop until the expected value is provided by the user. For example:

```
$ read name
joe doe
$ while [ "$name" != 'whoami' ]
> do
>      echo "wrong name, does not match login name"
>      read name
> done
wrong name
joe doe
wrong name
rodney
$
```

Until the input provided in bold matches the results of executing the command **whoami**, this loop continues forever. Also, notice that the value of the variable **$name** is stored in double quotes. This is important because the double quotes store the value of the variable as a string literal for proper processing by the **while** command. Double quotes also allow the value of a variable to be displayed instead of the variable name.

Now let us take a look at combining positional parameters with the **for** construct:

$0 is the first positional parameter (the command/script name)
$# contains the number of positional parameters or arguments
$* stores all of the positional parameters

In the following example we set the command list to include four colors. Each value is stored in the built-in variable **$***. The **for** loop is used to loop through each value in the list and displays it (each color) on the screen:

```
$ set red yellow blue gray
$ for i in $*
> do
> echo $i
> done
red
yellow
blue
```

gray

The next example simply displays the number of strings stored in the positional parameter list "$#":

$ echo $#
4

Finally, the $0, $1, $2, $3, and $4 variables are displayed individually to show each element contained in the list:

$ echo $0 $1 $2 $3 $4
/bin/sh red yellow blue gray

Notice that the first argument is actually the value of the shell itself. If we had created a shell script called **print_values**, the string "print_values" would have been displayed for the variable $0.

Exercise 6

1 Use the **while** looping expression to continue
  looping until the user enters a string that
  matches the home directory provided by the
  Bourne shell **$HOME** environment variable.

6.7 SETTING AND UNSETTING VARIABLES

To set a built-in environment variable in the UNIX Bourne shell, the **set** command is not necessary. The **set** command is required for creating and assigning values to local and environment variables in the C shell. To change the built-in shell environment variable for the terminal type, use the following command for the Bourne shell:

$ TERM=wyse

Remember that unless we also use the **export** command afterward, the environment variable will not be updated for all child processes that are created. For example, if the user starts another shell using the **sh** command, that child shell will not know about this setting (our terminal type). Local variables can be

created and set as follows:

$ local_variable=rodney

To see all environment variables, you can use the **set** command. To clear the assignment of the variable, use the **unset** command, as follows:

$ unset local_variable

To check that the variable has been **unset,** you can also use the **echo** command followed by the local variable name. Make sure to include the dollar sign before the variable name!

6.8   VARIABLE SUBSTITUTION

Variables can be assigned default values when no value exists. The following example checks to see if the variable **drink** has been set. If it has not been set, the variable drink will be assigned the value "coffee":

```
$ echo ${drink:-coffee}
coffee
$ set drink=tea
$ echo ${drink:-coffee}
tea
```

After we assign a value to the variable **drink,** we use the **echo** statement to determine what will be displayed. When the default case is no longer true, the **echo** command displays the value "tea" for the drink variable. The following command permanently assigns a default value to the variable **user** if it has not been assigned a value (is undefined):

```
$ echo ${user:='whoami'}
rodney
```

The next example checks that the HOME environment variable is set and is nonnull. If it is not set it will print the message "We have no HOME":

```
$ echo ${HOME:?"We have no HOME"}
/mnt/rodney
```

In the above example my HOME environment variable is set to the value of **/mnt/rodney**. If a user does not have a HOME environment variable set, you want to make sure it is set (many shell scripts rely upon the HOME environment variable's value).

The last example shows what happens when a variable is assigned a value that is nonnull. The shell replaces the old value with a new value; otherwise, a null (empty) value is displayed:

```
$ echo ${foobar:+newvalue}
$ foobar=joe
$ echo ${foobar:+bill}
bill
```

In the first case, nothing is displayed because the variable is null. In the second case, the new value is assigned (**foobar=bill**), because the variable **foobar** has previously been assigned (has a value).

Exercise 7

1 Use variable substitution to assign a default value to a variable called **username**. This default value should always be set to the current name, as providde by the **whoami** command.

2 Display the contents of the variable **username**.

3 How can you clear the contents of the variable?

6.9 THE EXPR COMMAND

If is often useful to perform arithmetic operations in Bourne shell scripts. Many shell scripts often need to keep a loop counter to determine the number of cycles executed. Counting loops is often useful when test scripts are used to test product reliability (i.e., the number of cycles performed before an error occurs). The following script attempts to loop four times and calculate the number of successful loops each time by incrementing a counter variable called **loop_count**:

```
$ loop_count=1
$ while [ $loop_count -lt 4 ]
> do
```

```
>      echo $loop_count
>      loop_count='expr $loop_count + 1'
> done
1
2
3
```

Exercise 8

1 What command can you use to calculate values?

2 Write a shell script to calculate and display the
   number to attempts required to complete Exercise 6. For review, Exercise 6 required the user to
   enter the proper value for the HOME environment variable directory setting. This exercise
   also continued looping until a proper name
   (match) was found.

6.10 THE CASE STATEMENT

The **case** statement allows conditional execution of statements based
upon a string match. This is one of the best methods for processing command line
arguments. For example, the **ls** command has many options (i.e., **-l, -R, -a**). The
case statement is often the most efficient and effective method of writing a shell
script procedure to evaluate a set or group of command-line options. The following
example evaluates and displays all valid options that have been provided (i.e., **-a,
-b**):

```
echo "Enter a command"
read option
case "$option" in
a)
      echo "The a option was selected"
b)
      echo "The b option was selected"
*)
      echo "Invalid option was selected"
esac
```

This script expects that the user will enter either the character "a" or "b"; otherwise, the message "Invalid option was selected" will be displayed. This message is also called the default case. The * matches anything else that is supplied as input.

Exercise 9

1 Write a shell script to prompt the user to enter the letter "l", "p", or "w". Next, execute the appropriate command, as follows (use the **case** statement):

l Execute the **ls** command

p Execute the **pwd** command

w Execute the **whoami** command

If an input other than the previous input is provided, display the message "Invalid command request". Put this script inside a loop and add the letter "q" to quit the program using the **exit** command.

6.11 THE SHIFT COMMAND

The **shift** command is useful for processing many argument or command-line options. It shifts all arguments in the list to the left one position. In the following example, we **echo** each value that is left in the list until there are no more values left:

```
$ set one two three four five
$ while [ $# -gt 0 ]
> do
>       echo $*
>       shift
>done
one two three four five
two three four five
three four five
four five
five
```

Exercise 10

1 What command processes arguments contained in a list?

2 Write a shell script to display the tenth and eleventh strings contained in the following list of possible values: a b c d e f g h i j k l.

6.12 FUNCTIONS

Shell functions are one of the most powerful features available with the Bourne shell (not available with the C shell). Execution of a function is faster than file execution because the search path does not have to be evaluated by the shell. Another benefit of functions is that they provide return values that can be provided to the calling program to determine execution success or failure. The dot command reads functions and definitions stored in a file for use by other programs. It is also helpful to include commonly used functions in the user's **.profile** file located in the home directory. Placing commonly used commands in **.profile** so each function always is available after log in is very important. The following function **myinfo** is contained in the file **myfunctions**:

```
myinfo ()
{
echo "The date and time is" `date`
echo "Your currently logged in as " `whoami`
echo "Your HOME directory is $HOME"
}
```

First, we must read the file **myfunctions** using the Bourne shell's dot command to make the function available to our shell, as follows:

$. myfunctions

Now we can simply execute the function info directly from the shell as follows without having to execute a file or program:

$ info
The date and time is Tue Aug 30 14:24:35 PDT 1994
Your currently logged in as rodney
Your HOME directory is /mnt/rodney

Exercise 11

1 Create a function that displays your current
   working directory, primary and secondary
   prompts, search path, and **login** name. Call this
   function in your program.

2 Include text along with each output for proper
   identification of what is being displayed by the
   function during execution.

6.13 TRAP HANDLERS

It is often useful to include a *trap handler* in your shell script. A trap handler allows you (the programmer) to predefine how your program (shell script) deals with predefined events (signals). You can use the **stty** command to display the various signal definitions defined for your current shell. For example, the interrupt signal is normally set to a control C. This means that if you want to interrupt a program during execution, you must hold down the control and C keys together (either lowercase or uppercase C). This key sequence will interrupt or **kill** the current executing program. A trap handler may be required if you are in the middle of a critical function and require the user to complete an operation before terminating. Normally, if the user enters a control C, the program will simply terminate; however, if a trap handler is defined, you can send a warning message to the user via the trap handler and continue processing. The following shell script **myloop** does not terminate if a control C is provided; however, this program exits when the **exit** command is provided:

```
$ cat myloop
            #!/bin/sh
trap continue 2
while true
> do
      echo "enter some text"
      read input
      if [ "$input" = "exit" ]
      then
      break
      fi
done
```

$ **myloop**
enter some text
Hello how are you?
enter some text
^C
enter some text
exit

It should also be pointed out that there is another signal that can be used to terminate programs. The abort signal can be sent using the control and back-slash ("\") keys together (usual **stty** setting for abort). This signal also causes the shell to create a file called **core** in the current working directory. The **core** file contains a snapshot of memory and is commonly used for debugging the program using **dbx, sdb,** or **adb.**

Exercise 12

1 Create a shell script that continuously prompts for a user name, phone, and fax number. Store these data in a file called **employee_info**. Add a trap handler to the shell script (control C) to ensure that the user cannot simply terminate the program in the middle of processing. This is especially important, because you do not want the user to end up with part of an address or phone number in a database or output file (**employee_info**). At the end of input for a user, prompt the user if more data are to be entered. If not, let the user exit the program.

2 What are some other potential signals that could interrupt our program during execution?

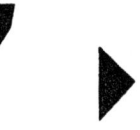

chapter 7 ▶

The C Shell

*T*he C shell extends many of the functions of the Bourne shell to provide even greater efficiency and productivity. This chapter provides many more examples and exercises to help supplement the learning process for the UNIX C shell. Again, it is recommended that the user have a computer running the UNIX operating system. It is also advised that either the hard-copy or on-line man page for the **csh** (C shell) be used along with the following exercises. The following features of the C shell are discussed in this chapter:

- Metacharacters and the **history** function
- Input and output file redirection
- Conditional command expressions
- Double and single quotes
- Aliases
- Reading input into a variable
- Looping constructs
- History substitution

7.1 METACHARACTERS AND THE HISTORY FUNCTION

The C shell provides all of the same metacharacters as the Bourne shell. For example:

\	Escape special meaning of a metacharacter
&	Execute a program in the background
;	Separate multiple commands on a single line
$	The contents of a variable (i.e., echo $HOME)
?	Match a single character with any value
*	Match zero or more characters with any value
[a-c]	Match the letters a through c

The C shell provides one new metacharacter for **history**. The exclamation point , "!", is used to repeat previous commands in the C shell's history buffer. One of the greatest difficulties with the Bourne shell is that you cannot repeat a command without typing in the entire line a second time. The **history** facility solves this problem. To start storing commands for reuse, first set the size of the **history** buffer to hold previous commands. For example, if we wanted to always store the last 50 commands that have been entered, type in:

% set history=50

Notice that my prompt also now has changed from the dollar sign (used in the previous chapter for the Bourne shell) to a percent sign. Now the question is, what will happen if you enter more than 50 commands after using the preceding command? For example, after you enter the 51st command, the first command disappears from the history buffer.

After you tell the C shell how many commands you want to store in the **history** buffer, you can begin saving commands. To review your previous commands, enter the following command:

% history
1 ls
2 history
3 cat foobar

To repeat the first command, we simply need to specify the command number. In this case, the first command is selected from our **history** buffer, as follows:

```
% !1
ls
myfiles          people          query
rodney           scott           tom
```

You can also use the **history** metacharacter "!" followed by a unique string for the last command you want to execute again. The following example reexecutes the last command that started with the letter "c" (i.e., the **cat** command):

```
% !c
cat foobar
This is the contents of the foobar file.
This is the end of the foobar file.
```

Notice that only the first character was required after the **history** metacharacter. This is because the **cat** command was the only command that started with the letter c in our history buffer.

Exercise 1

1 Establish a **history** buffer that can store at least 100 commands.

2 Use the **history** metacharacter to repeat the last command that was used to list the contents of a directory.

3 How can you repeat this same command using the command number instead of the first part of the command name?

4 What command repeats the command prior to the previous command (using a command number and not symbolic representation)?

7.2   INPUT AND OUTPUT FILE REDIRECTION

The C shell provides the same input and output redirection facilities as the Bourne shell. However, redirection to standard error and standard output is

different. The following command sends both error messages as well as output to the file **error_log**:

% **ls >& error_log**

Another feature provided by the C shell is **noclobber**. This feature prevents writing on top of an existing file when using output file redirection. Therefore, if a file already exists and you attempt to redirect output while the **noclobber** variable is set, the following error will occur:

% **cat > existing_file**
existing_file: File exists.

To override the **noclobber** feature, use the exclamation point (also known as the "bang" character) after the redirection symbol, as follows:

% **cat foobar >! existing_file**

Using the **cat** command to redirect output from one file to another has the same effect as copying the file **foobar** to **existing_file**. Using the append version of redirection, ">>", does not require the exclamation point to turn off the **noclobber** feature because we are only appending to the file, not overwriting the contents.

7.3 COMMAND CONDITIONAL EXPRESSIONS

The "&&" (conditional and) command expression can be used to evaluate the success of the first command to the left of the "&&" operator. If the first command is successful, the shell will execute the command on the right of the "&&". The following example evaluates the success of the **cp** command. If the command is successful, it will send **mail** to **rodney** that the copy was successful:

% **cp oldfile newfile && (echo "cp success" || mail rodney)**

The "||" (conditional or) command expression is the opposite of the conditional and operator "&&". If the first command fails, the second command to the right of the conditional or "||" will be executed. This can be useful for error reporting. For example:

% **cp oldfile newfile >& errors || mail rodney < errors**

> ### Exercise 2
>
> 1 Use the conditional and operator "&&" to check if
>   the return status from exiting the **vi** editor was
>   successful. If so, use the **write** command to write
>   a status message to yourself explaining this con-
>   dition.
>
> 2 Send yourself an error message using **mail** if you
>   are unable to **write** to a user that is currently not
>   logged into the system.

7.4 DOUBLE AND SINGLE QUOTES

Single quotes must be matched on a single line (unless the back-slash key
is used). Single quotes provide the ability to hide all characters except the history
metacharacter, "!". The following two examples show both conditions:

> % **echo 'The C shell requires a matching single quote**
> Unmatched '.
> % **echo 'The exclamation point must be escaped !'**
> Unmatched '.
> % **echo "Use the \ to escape the exclamation point - hello\!"**
> Use the \ to escape the exclamation point - hello!

The single back quote is used to execute the contents of the string as a
command and provide the output as a string literal. The following example displays the results of executing the date command as a string literal:

> % **echo "The date is "'date'**
> The date is Wed Aug 31 10:17:49 PDT 1994

The double quotes also must be matched on a single line, unless the back-
slash character is used to continue the line. The double quotes are unique in that
they can be used for variable substitution. The following example displays the contents of the environment variable **HOME**:

> % **echo "My home is $HOME"**
> My home is /usr/mnt/rodney

Notice what happens when we use the single quotes:

% **echo 'My home is $HOME'**
My home is $HOME

The back-slash character does not work for the dollar sign character in the C shell:

% **echo "The cost is \$1.00"**
The cost is \.00

The shell thinks that $1 is a variable; however, it does not exist. The back-slash is also displayed because we have placed it inside the double quotes. The same condition of escaping the special meaning of the back-slash character can be provided by placing two back-slash characters together (i.e., a back-slash back-slash character sequence). One way to resolve the problem of displaying a dollar sign as a string literal is to use single quotes:

% **echo 'The cost is $1.00'**
The cost is $1.00

Exercise 3

1 How can you hide the special meaning of the following text characters in a string: *, &, |, ?, $?

2 How can you create a file called **?mark?**

3 How can you delete the file **?mark?**

4 How can you display the settings for the following C shell environment variables: **home, term, path, prompt?**

5 What command displays "My log in name is" and the results of the **login** program all on the same line?

7.5 ALIASES

Another useful feature available only in the C shell is aliases. An **alias** allows the user to construct an alternate, or **alias**, name for a command or series of commands. To display your current set of **alias** assignments, use the following command:

```
% alias
a      alias
d      dirs
l      (ls -F)
pd     pushd
po     popd
cd     'cd \!*; set prompt="$cwd > " '
```

The first **alias** defines the command **a** as an equivalent command to **alias**. The second **alias** lists executable files with a trailing "*", links with a trailing "@", and directories with a trailing "/". The next two aliases shorten the command for pushing and popping directories on the directory stack to just **pd** and **po**. The **pushd** or **pd** command saves the current directory location on a stack. After we have used the command **pd,** we can change to a new location using the **cd** command and then issue the command **popd** or **po** and return to the last directory saved on the stack (i.e., where the last **pd** command was performed). The **dirs or d** command also can be used to display the directory stack. It is often nice to have the shell display your current working directory as a prompt. This eliminates the need to continue to enter the **pwd** command all the time. The last **alias** changes the **cd** command so that it does not only change directories to the directory path provided as an argument, but then sets the prompt to equal to our new current working directory. It is also suggested that you set the prompt environment variable in your **.cshrc** file, so that the current working directory is displayed at your first initial prompt:

% alias cd cd \!*; set prompt = "$cwd>"

Exercise 4
1 Create an **alias** that performs a recursive list of all subdirectories encountered (use the short name **lr** for this **alias**).

Exercise 4 (Continued)

2 Create another **alias** that pipes the output of a recursive **ls** to the **more** command. (The **more** command allows you to see information on a page-by-page basis.) Use the name **lrm** for this **alias**.

3 Update your prompt each time to display not only your current working directory, but also your host name first, followed by a colon.

7.6   READING INPUT INTO VARIABLES

Shell scripts often include interactive commands (i.e., where a prompt requests the user to answer a question and store the answer in a variable). You should include the following string as the first line in your C shell script to tell the current executing shell you want to execute this script under the control of the C shell, not the Bourne shell or any other shell:

#!/bin/csh

A special C shell variable is used to read input from the keyboard into a variable. The following example asks the user to enter his or her name and phone number on one line. All data entered up to the first carriage return are stored in the variable user_info:

```
#!/bin/csh
start:
echo "Enter your name"
set user_info = $<
echo "Your name is "
echo $user_info
echo "Enter y if this is correct"
set answer = $<
if "$answer" != "y" then
      goto start
endif
```

Exercise 5

1 Create a C shell script that prompts the user for his or her name and home phone number, redisplays the information, and confirms that all data entered are still correct. If the information is not correct, allow the user to reenter the information until all data are acceptable. (This program can be very valuable for creating a database of information that is extremely useful.)

2 What other information may be important to store in this database?

7.7 LOOPING CONSTRUCTS

The C shell provides looping constructs similar to the Bourne shell; however, instead of the **for** statement, the C shell uses the **foreach** command. The **foreach** statement loops through a list of elements and assigns the "file" variable a value from each member in the list (all the files in the current working directory in this case because "*" is used):

```
% foreach file ( 'ls *' )
?      echo -n "Do you want to "; rm -i $file
? end
```

Notice the **-n** option is used with the **echo** command. This causes **echo** not to send a new line and carriage return after displaying the results. The results of execution of the preceding command follow:

```
Do you want to rm: remove a? n
Do you want to rm: remove b? y
Do you want to rm: remove c? n
Do you want to rm: remove check_for_file? n
Do you want to rm: remove d? n
```

The results of this operation (removing and not removing specific files) can be verified using the **ls** command, as follows:

```
% ls
a    c          check_for_file d
```

Notice that the file **b** has been removed by the **rm** command.

The **while** loop is very similar to the **foreach** loop; however, looping terminates when the **while** condition becomes false. The following shell script loops and continues the loop until either the user guesses the correct number (the users process id) or gives up and enters the string "quit":

```
#!/bin/csh
set number = $$
echo "Enter a number or quit"
set answer = $<
while ( "$answer" != "$number" )
        if "$answer" == "quit" then
                break
        endif
        echo "try again?"
        set answer = $<
end
```

Notice that the **if** condition in the C shell uses the double equals to compare to values; however, in the Bourne shell, only a single equals sign is used.

Exercise 6

1 Create a **foreach** loop to check with the user to see if a backup of each file in the current directory is required. Use the **cp** command to copy the file to the same source name with a ".bak" file extension appended.

2 Now create a program with a **while** loop that continues looping for input until an "n" is entered on a line by itself. At the end of the program, display all input that was provided. Note, it is often helpful for debugging purposes to include the "-x" flag at the end of the first "#!/bin/csh" command in your shell script. This special flag tells the shell to display each command during execution. This can be a very helpful for debugging purposes (i.e., each command is displayed as it is executed by the C shell).

7.8 THE HISTORY SUBSTITUTION FACILITY

One of the major benefits of the **history** function is not only the capability of repeating previous commands, but modification of a command prior execution. The **ksh** (Korn shell) provides a method to repeat previous commands; however, the screen interface is based upon commands from the **vi** editor or the **fc** command. The C shell's method of command substitution is not as friendly as the **ksh**; however, the C shell is still much better than having to retype an entire command, especially if the command is long, awkward, and cumbersome.

The **history** command allows the user to repeat a previous command stored in the **history** buffer. For review, the following command repeats the last command that started with the letter "l":

    % !l
    ls
    a   c   check_for_file d

Before discussing how to use quick substitution, it is useful to discuss the print-only feature to the **history** feature. To just display a command without executing it from the history buffer, use the **:p** command. The following example shows how to display the last command that started with the letter "l" without actually executing the command:

    % !l:p
    ls -a -l -R

In the preceding example, the last command to start with the letter "l" was the **ls** command; however, this command invocation included three options (all, long, and recursive). Using the **history** substitution facility, we can change one or more of these options. For example, to change the command so that we do not display all files **-a** (displays hidden files or files that start with a period) and instead display the group for each file, execute the following:

    % ^-a^-g^
    ls -g -l -R
    -rw-r--r-- 1 rodney instructor   0 Aug 29 16:53 a
    -rw-r--r-- 1 rodney instructor   0 Aug 29 16:53 c

The key to **history** (quick) substitution is to make sure to select a unique string as the target or original command for substitution. The source string to change must be surrounded by the caret, "^". Next, you must provide the string or

strings that you want to use as replacements. Alternatively, you can provide nothing. This removes the original string from the previous command. The last circumflex is not required unless you want to remove part of a previous command. The following example locates and prints (not execute) the last **ls** command from our **history** buffer. Next, we eliminate the -R option:

```
% !ls:p
ls -a -l -R
<output not shown>
% ^-a -l -R^^
ls
<output not shown>
```

Exercise 7

1　Enter the command to copy a file from one name to a new name.

2　Use the **vi** editor to edit the new file.

3　Finally, use the history quick substitution character to change the file name for both the **cp** and **vi** commands.

chapter *8* ▶

Advanced UNIX Commands

*T*he UNIX operating system provides a plethora of commands and tools. This chapter provides many examples and exercises, with the continued belief that examples and practice exercises are the best way to learn new concepts (especially UNIX commands). Many commands have already been provided and used in previous chapters. This chapter continues to build upon the foundation of knowledge obtained from experience gained through the study of previous chapters. The following commands are discussed:

- The **sort** command
- The **find** command
- The Stream Editor (**sed**)
- Pattern scanning and processing with **awk**

8.1   THE SORT COMMAND

The **sort** command has been used in previous chapters to help filter data by taking input and sorting it in ascending order (by default). The **sort** command provides many other functions:

% **sort file1**   Output data to the screen in ascending order, not change to file "file1"

% **sort -nr**   Sort data using numerical values and reverse the order (largest numbers first)

Using the preceding **sort** options, we can perform many useful filtering operations, for example, sorting output provided by the **du** command (disk usage). The **du** command displays the amount of disk space consumed for all files and directories contained in the current or specified working directory. The -s option summarizes or provides a grand total for each file. Using this option, the user can combine both commands into a pipeline to identify users that are consuming the most amount of disk space:

% **du -s | sort -nr**

This is just one of many commands that UNIX system administrators use to monitor critical system resources, such as hard disk space. The following command displays the sorted disk usage summary results for four directories:

% **du -s StP T3.1 castillo t4.0 | sort -nr**
```
177917       StP
28495        t4.0
8659         castillo
3886         T3.1
```

The **StP** directory (user) is clearly the largest consumer of disk space, followed by the **t4.0** directory.

Exercise 1

1 Use the **du** command together with the **sort** command to identify heavy disk space users on your system.

2 If you are fortunate enough to not have to share your disk with others, identify the files in your directory that are the largest consumers of your precious disk space.

8.2 THE FIND COMMAND

The **find** command provides many options for searching for files on your UNIX system. The following flags are frequently used.

- Finds files that match the name **foobar** starting from the current working directory:

  % find . -name foobar

- Finds files in the **/tmp** directory with read, write, and execute permissions for the owner, read-only permission for members of the group, and write and execute permissions for other users:

  % find /tmp -perm 743

- Displays all files and directories that start with a J starting from the current working directory (notice that the metacharacter must always be escaped):

  % find . -name "J*" -print

- For each match, changes the permissions for read, write, and execute for all:

  % find . -name "J*" -exec chmod 777 {} \;

- Finds files that are owned by rodney starting from the current working directory:

  % find . -name "*" -user rodney

- Finds all files (in the **/tmp** directory) modified in the last 3 days. This flag is useful for pruning or removing old accounting and temporary files:

  % find /tmp -name ".*" -mtime 3

- Finds directories "d", block special "b", character special "c", plain files "f", named pipes "p", symbolic links "l", and sockets "s" using the **-type** option. The following example finds all directories from the current working directory and below:

  % find . -type d

Block special files are usually associated with the hard disk device and are used for devices that contain a file system. A block special file provides buffering of data through the UNIX file system. A *character special* file does not provide any buffering and usually is associated with devices such as the keyboard, display, printer, and other nonrandom-access devices. Several UNIX database software vendors prefer not to use the UNIX block device (file system). Instead, they often per-

form their own input and output operations using the physical hard disk (raw or character device). Using this device improves performance and bypasses the overhead required by the UNIX file system code provided by the kernel. Character special device files are also known as *raw devices* because they can only perform direct input and output to a device. *Named pipes* provide communications between processes for exchange of data. *Symbolic links* were discussed in previous chapters as used to create a pointer between two files located on different file systems. Finally, a *socket* provides an end point of communication between two processes (programs during execution).

The following example helps to better demonstrate the power and use of the **find** command. The first example shows how to locate all files that have the file extension ".bak" from the current working directory and all subdirectories:

% find . -name "*.bak" -print

The asterisk must be escaped using either double quotes or back-slash characters. The next example prints all zero-length files. After three files (**a, b, c**) are displayed, the next command deletes all zero-length files from the current working directory. This command also can be considered a pruning function (it increases the number of available file system inodes):

% find . -size 0 -print
./a
./c
./d
% find . -size 0 -exec rm {} \;
% find . -size 0 -print

Notice that the **rm** command did remove the zero-length files **a, c,** and **d,** as verified by the third and final **find** command. The following example is useful for finding files that are relatively large (5000 characters) and have not been accessed in over 90 days. It uses the interactive option of the **rm** command to ask the user if the user wants to remove the files. Even if the user enters "y", he or she must have write permission to successfully remove a file:

% find . -type f -size +5000c -atime +90 -ok rm -i {} \;

The **-ok** option is necessary because we are going to execute the **rm** command with the **-i** option for interactive confirmation of any file removal. The interactive option causes the command to read input and expect a "y" response as input prior to deleting the file. The **-f** option to **rm** can be used instead of **-i** to force removal. The force option causes error messages and warnings not to be displayed, so be careful with this option, even though you still must have write permission to the file to delete.

The next example demonstrates the or option to the **find** command. This function is useful for selecting multiple-file types (e.g., either a plain file or directory, as shown can be specified):

> % **find . \(-type f -o -type d \) -print**
>
> .
> ./fj
> ./check_for_file

The parentheses are escaped using the back slash because we do not want to confuse the shell and have it think that we want part of the command to be executed by a single subshell. The following example runs the **find** command as a subshell and sends the output of the results to our display device. Error messages are redirected to an error log file. This command starts from the top of the UNIX directory hierarchy and traverses the entire directory structure (hierarchy).

> % (**find / -name "*.tst" -print) >& error_log**
> < no results >
> % (**find / -name "*.tst" -print > 'tty') >& /tmp/error_log**
> ./fi.tst
> ./foo.tst

Redirecting output from the **find** command using the **tty** command in the previous command is important. This is required because the parentheses result in command execution by a subshell. The command subshell does not have an associated device for output (i.e., a display device). Therefore, the output is often lost in the first case and is displayed on the current output device in the second.

Exercise 2

1 What command displays all files and directories of size zero?

2 How can you make sure that you specify all files and directories from the top of the UNIX hierarchy, not just those entries that are in your home or current working directory?

Exercise 2 *(Continued)*

3 Create a shell script to prune all files in your home directory and all subdirectories that are zero-length or have the name **core**. Use a modification time of 5 days or longer.

4 Add to your command the ability to remove object files (files that end in the ".o" file extension). Your system administrator may also like to have a copy of your prune script so as to eliminate systemwide accounting files from the **cron, uucp, lp,** and other programs. The **cron** program is used to schedule execution of programs at a future date and time. The **uucp** program is used for UNIX-to-UNIX copying of files between machines. The **lp** command is used to send a file to the line printer.

8.3   THE STREAM EDITOR (SED)

The **sed** command is used to perform editing in a batch, rather than in an interactive mode. In other words, it allows you to edit a file from a shell script, rather than having to use the **vi** editor interactively. The following example helps to explain some of the many features available with the **sed** command:

% sed '1,5d' myfile > mynewfile	Deletes the first five lines of the file **myfile** and redirects changes to **mynewfile**
% sed '/[Mo,Fa]ther/d' myfile	Deletes or does not display all lines that contain the string Mother or Father. Note that this command does not change the contents of the source file **myfile**
% sed 's/^/?/' mail1 > response	Places a "?" in front of each line of text for a mail message that was just received
% sed 's/.//' response	Removes each "?" from the front of each line in the file.

Exercise 3

1 Use the **sed** command to delete the first five lines (typically, the **mail** header) in the file **mailfile**.

2 Edit the file so that each line starts with the special character ">".

3 Reverse the process so that the special character contained at the beginning of each line is removed.

4 Use the **write** command "w" inside the stream editor to copy the file **myfile** to **/tmp/sed.exercise**.

8.4 PATTERN SCANNING AND PROCESSING WITH AWK

The **awk** command is a language unto itself. It received its name after the first letter of the authors' last names were combined (i.e., Aho, Weinberger, and Kernighan). It uses the following database primitives for processing complex commands:

FS   Field separator (colon, space, tab, etc.)
NF   Number of fields in the data file
RS   Record separator (new line usually)
OFS   Output field separator (single space usually)

The **/etc/passwd** file can be used to demonstrate the capabilities of the **awk** command. The following command displays the contents of my local copy of the **/etc/passwd** file:

% **cat mypasswd**
root:*:0:1:Operator - Rodney Wilson:/:/bin/csh
nobody:*:65534:65534::/:
daemon:*:1:1::/:
sys:*:2:2::/:/bin/csh
bin:*:3:3::/bin:
uucp:*:4:8::/var/spool/uucppublic:
news:*:6:6::/var/spool/news:/bin/csh
ingres:*:7:7::/usr/ingres:/bin/csh

```
audit:*:9:9::/etc/security/audit:/bin/csh
sync::1:1::/:/bin/sync
dtet::1234:12:TET:/usr/mnt/rodney/dtet2.2.2/src:/bin/csh
tet::1234:12:TET:/usr/mnt/rodney/dtet2.2.2/src:/bin/csh
+::0:0:::
```

Now using the preceding data from **mypasswd** file, several examples are provided to help demonstrate the capabilities of the **awk** command. The first example displays all accounts that are using the C shell (**csh**):

% awk -F: '/csh/' mypasswd
```
root:*:0:1:Operator - Rodney Wilson:/:/bin/csh
sys:*:2:2::/:/bin/csh
news:*:6:6::/var/spool/news:/bin/csh
ingres:*:7:7::/usr/ingres:/bin/csh
audit:*:9:9::/etc/security/audit:/bin/csh
dtet::1234:12:TET:/usr/mnt/rodney/dtet2.2.2/src:/bin/csh
tet::1234:12:TET:/usr/mnt/rodney/dtet2.2.2/src:/bin/csh
```

Notice that the field separator is defined as the colon, which is followed by the search string "csh". The next example also only displays accounts that use the **csh**; however, only the **login** name, user identification number (UID), and default shell are displayed (fields 1, 3, and 7):

% awk -F: '/csh/ {print $1, $3, $7}' mypasswd
```
root 0 /bin/csh
sys 2 /bin/csh
news 6 /bin/csh
ingres 7 /bin/csh
audit 9 /bin/csh
dtet 1234 /bin/csh
tet 1234 /bin/csh
```

Notice that the braces are required around the **print** statement. The **awk** command also provides the ability to compare values and only display lines that meet the search criteria. The following example displays **login** names that have a user id greater than 10:

% awk -F: '$3 > 10' mypasswd
```
nobody
dtet
tet
```

Another possibility is to select a range of values. If we wanted to print all accounts with a user id between 2 and 9, the following command could be used:

% awk -F: '$3 <= 9 && $3 >= 2' mypasswd
sys:*:2:2::/:/bin/csh
bin:*:3:3::/bin:
uucp:*:4:8::/var/spool/uucppublic:
news:*:6:6::/var/spool/news:/bin/csh
ingres:*:7:7::/usr/ingres:/bin/csh
audit:*:9:9::/etc/security/audit:/bin/csh

You can also use the **awk** command to display lines that do not have specific values for certain fields. The following command displays all accounts where the user id is not 4, 5, or 6:

% awk -F: '!($3 == 4 || $3 == 5 || $3 == 6)' mypasswd
root:*:0:1:Operator - Rodney Wilson:/:/bin/csh
nobody:*:65534:65534::/:
daemon:*:1:1::/:
sys:*:2:2::/:/bin/csh
bin:*:3:3::/bin:
ingres:*:7:7::/usr/ingres:/bin/csh
audit:*:9:9::/etc/security/audit:/bin/csh
sync::1:1::/:/bin/sync
dtet::1234:12:TET:/usr/mnt/rodney/dtet2.2.2/src:/bin/csh
tet::1234:12:TET:/usr/mnt/rodney/dtet2.2.2/src:/bin/csh
+::0:0:::

The next **awk** command displays the record number and the total number of records for each line in **mypasswd** file that do not use the **csh** as the default **login** shell:

% awk -F: '!($7 == "/bin/csh") {print NR, NF}' mypasswd
2 7
3 7
5 7
6 7
10 7
13 7

The number of characters for each line also can be displayed using the length variable; however, let us also increase the space between the **login** name

and the length using the tab as the Output Field Separator (OFS) instead of a space to make the results more easy to read (greater space between fields):

```
% awk -F: '{FS=":";OFS=""} {print length, $1}' mypasswd
46        root
24        nobody
16        daemon
21        sys
16        bin
34        uucp
36        news
34        ingres
41        audit
22        sync
56        dtet
55        tet
9 +
```

To display the summary of the number of accounts in the file, use the following:

```
% awk -F: 'END {print "Total accounts = "NR }' mypasswd
Total accounts = 13
```

Heading information can also be displayed with the output. In the following case, we want to ignore accounts that do not have a default **login** shell:

```
% awk -F: 'BEGIN{FS=":";OFS="\t"; \
print "\t Login Name \t \t Default Shell"; \
print " "} \
!($7 == "") {printf "\t %-6s \t \t %-10s\n",$1, $7}' mypasswd
          Login Name      Default Shell
          root            /bin/csh
          sys             /bin/csh
          news            /bin/csh
          ingres          /bin/csh
          audit           /bin/csh
          sync            /bin/sync
          dtet            /bin/csh
          tet             /bin/csh
```

Exercise 4

1 Copy and create your own private version of the /etc/passwd file.

2 Use the **awk** command to display each line in the file.

3 Now use the **awk** command to display lines in the file that do not have a password entry (the second field in the file). You should note that if you are using UNIX System V Release 4 (SVR4), you will need access to the **/etc/shadow** file from your system administrator; otherwise, use the comment field (field number 5).

4 Combine your **awk** script with a shell script that sends **mail** to all users informing them that they currently do not have a password.

5 Use the **awk** command's **printf** function to format all output fields contained in the **mypasswd** file. Create a heading line that explains each field (**login** name, comment, home directory, and default **login** shell). Make sure to use tabs so there is enough space between fields for both the heading as well as the record information. (This is very important and makes the output much more easy to read.) It is also important to note that the comment field in the **/etc/passwd** file is often neglected and yet can provide valuable information for other users, especially in the case of an emergency when you need to know how to contact a user at home. The **finger** command also provides this information (if configured).

chapter 9

Introduction
to Programming Tools

*T*he UNIX operating system was designed by programmers and software developers primarily for their use. As a new user to the UNIX operating system, you may now be thinking of UNIX as user-hostile instead of user-friendly. However, to the majority of experienced UNIX software engineers, it is one of the most efficient and effective operating systems available. One reason for this is that most commands are actually abbreviations for the facilities they provide. For example, the copy command is simply **cp**; to print the current working directory, type **pwd**. In fact, most UNIX commands are abbreviated names for the function they provide (to reduce both time and keystrokes)[*].

In this chapter, many examples and exercises are provided; however, the focus moves from user commands to programming tools. UNIX is mostly written in the C language. Most UNIX applications are also written in C. Therefore, this chapter deals exclusively with programming tools for the C language:

---

[*]UNIX engineers love to save time and keystrokes because they usually have too much work to complete and not enough time ;-).

- The C compiler
- The **make** command
- The Revision Control System (RCS)
- Libraries and the Application Binary Interface (ABI)

9.1 CONSTRUCTING BINARY EXECUTABLES

Before discussing the tools for construction and maintenance of C programs, a brief explanation is provided to describe how programs like **ls** and **cp** evolve.

The source file first must be created before you can compile the program. As mentioned before, most source files are usually written in C. The C language is also called a *high-level language*. This is because the instructions contained in the source file can be read and understood by humans (we hope). The contents of the source file must be compiled, assembled, and linked to create a file that can be machine-readable (executed by the computer).

The compilation process usually starts with a program called the *preprocessor*. The C preprocessor, **cpp**, performs many tasks (e.g., taking any include file definitions and making sure that they are properly incorporated into the program source code). Eventually, assembly language source code is created as output (processor-specific instructions). Next, the assembly language code is assembled by the assembler (**as**). Assembly language files always have a .s file extension and are microprocessor-specific (machine instructions). Therefore, these files are usually not portable from one microprocessor architecture to another without an instruction translator. The assembler creates (assembles) source code instructions into an object or machine-readable file. The object files can be linked with other objects or collections of object files called libraries. When the link editor, **ld**, command is finished linking (stitching together) all objects, a binary executable file is created. This file can be executed, just as you can execute the **ls** or **cat** command.

9.2 THE C COMPILER

The C compiler, **cc**, is used to create a binary executable file from a C language source code program. The C source code must be written according to rules and standards for the C programming language. The American National Standards Institute (ANSI) has created an ANSI-C standard. This standard provides a set of rules and conventions for programmers to follow when creating C pro-

grams. For example, the following C program displays the string "hello class" on the user's display:

```
main()
{
printf("hello class\n");
}
```

The first statement "main()" is required by the compiler to identify that this is the main entrance to the program and not a supporting function. The braces define a block of executable code statements. The open and close braces inside of main are always required (this defines a block). The semicolon at the end of the **printf** (the only real executable statement in the program) is also required for statement termination, much like the carriage return from the shell.

This program uses a standard function for printing (**printf**) that is contained in a standard C library (**libc**). The C compiler, by default, always link edits (**ld**) with functions from **libc**. Remember that a library is simply a collection of object files that contain various functions (e.g., **printf** to format data for printing on the user's display). Therefore, to compile the C program **myfile.c**, we only need to type the following (the -l option would be required if a library other than the standard C library **libc** was required):

% cc myfile.c

By default, the C compiler creates a file called **a.out.** This program can now be executed as follows:

% a.out
hello class

The results of executing the program are defined by the source code program (i.e., print the string "hello class"). We could have used the **-o** option, which is one of many C compiler command-line options. This option creates the **binary** executable file with a name other than **a.out** as specified by the user. A binary file is machine-specific and contains data that are in base 2 (i.e., a binary value of either 0 or 1). The following example compiles the program contained in **myfile.c** and creates an executable binary file called **hello:**

% cc myfile.c -o hello

Exercise 1

1 Check and see if you have a C compiler installed in your system by using the **cc** command to compile your own copy of **myfile.c**.

2 You can use the **man** command to review options provided by your C compiler.

3 How can you compile the myfile.c program so the executable is called **myprog** instead of the default (**a.out**)?

9.3   THE MAKE COMMAND

The **make** command allows software developers to maintain, update, and regenerate programs and files. This command expects to find a file called **Makefile** or **makefile** in the current working directory (by default). The following file contains a set of rules that are commonly used by the **make** command. By simply typing **make** at the shell prompt, the default rules defined in the file **Makefile** are executed. This is similar to the UNIX shell executing a shell script; each line in the file **makefile** or **Makefile** is read and executed by the **make** program. Many programmers define rules for clean, compile, and execute operations in their **makefile** or **Makefile**. A sample **Makefile** follows:

```
# Makefile
CC=cc

SOURCES=main.c triangle.c

OBJECTS=main.o triangle.o

triag: $(OBJECTS)
        $(CC) -o $@ $(OBJECTS)
main.o: main.c
        $(CC) -O -c main.c
triangle.o: triangle.c
        $(CC) -O -c triangle.c
```

```
clean:
# Sometimes there are too many file names for the rm command
# Therefore, the files have been split into two invocations
          rm -f hits fmap map tally *.A *.M
          rm -f *.out $(OBJECTS) errgen.* sims


clobber:
# See the comment for the clobber target
          rm -f triag hits fmap map tally *.A *.M
          rm -f *.out $(OBJECTS)
```

All **Makefile's** (just like shell scripts) use the pound character to represent a comment line. These lines are not executed by the **make** program and are only for reference. The default rules (commands) for this **Makefile** are to compile two programs: **main.c** and **triangle.c**. When both programs have successfully compiled and created object files **main.o** and **triangle.o** (defined by the -c option), the triag rule creates a single executable file called **triag**. The string $@ is defined as the name of the current target; in this case, this file name is **triag**. To remove all temporary files, use the command **make clean**. The command **make clobber** also removes the existing executable file called **triag**.

Exercise 2

1 Create your own **makefile** to compile your program **myfile.c**.

2 Add a rule to your program called "clean" that removes the object and executable file.

3 If you call your **makefile** something other than **mymakefile**, what option will you need to give to the **make** command to use your file?

4 Include rules to remove all object and temporary files when the target "clean" is used. Also, add a "clobber" target that removes the binary executable file name.

9.4 REVISION CONTROL SYSTEM (RCS)

The Revision Control System (**rcs**) provides the ability for multiple software developers to work together on the same file or program at the same time. This is important because each developer must be able to work with others, without destroying the other developer's work. One of the biggest challenges with any multiuser operating system is the management and coordination of files and directories using shared hard disk resources. For example, if two users open a file for editing at the same time, a problem can occur; the first user will write and quit out of the editor; however, their changes will have not been noticed by the other user. When the second user performs a write and quit from the editor, the changes will overwrite or disregard any changes made by the first user. To overcome this problem the UNIX operating system provides a Revision Control System, or **rcs**, for BSD-based systems. Alternatively, the Source Code Control System, or **sccs**, was originally available for System V—based UNIX systems (also has been ported to BSD). Both systems use a method called *file locking* to manage changes. File locking requires the user to obtain an exclusive file lock before the file can be opened with write permission. The process starts by first creating a directory called **RCS** in your current working directory. Next, the check in command, **ci**, is used to install the initial version of a file for RCS control, as follows:

```
% mkdir RCS
% ci myfile.c
RCS/myfile.c,v <-- myfile.c
initial revision: 1.1
enter description, terminated with ^D or '.':
NOTE: This is NOT the log message!
>> This is the first version of myfile.c
>> .
% ls RCS
myfile.c,v
% ls myfile.c
myfile.c not found
```

The **rlog** command is used to review your comments regarding each change (i.e., check in).

After the file **myfile.c** has been checked in to the RCS directory, it no longer exists in the current working directory. Also notice that the file now has a **,v** file extension added to its original name and is now located in the **RCS** directory. At this point, the file **myfile.c** can be checked out of the **RCS** directory for read-only access using the **co** command. Alternatively, you can check out the file

for read/write permission using the lock -l flag to **co**. The following example shows the difference between check out without a lock and check out with a lock:

```
% co myfile.c
RCS/myfile.c,v --> myfile.c
revision 1.1
done
% ls -l myfile.c
-r--r--r-- 1 rodney 36 Sep 6 15:23 myfile.c
% co -l myfile.c
RCS/myfile.c,v --> myfile.c
revision 1.1 (locked)
done
% ls -l myfile.c
-rw-r--r-- 1 rodney 36 Sep 6 15:24 myfile.c
```

Notice that after the file is checked out with a lock, user rodney now has write access to the file **myfile.c**. This prevents two users from overwriting each other's changes. However, until user rodney checks in the file back to the RCS system, no other users can check out the file with a lock, or make any changes.

Exercise 3

1 Create an RCS directory in your home directory and check in your **myfile.c** program. (Don't forget to also check in your **Makefile** that you created in the previous exercise.) It is always a good idea to include multiple lines of comments during the initial check in. For example, you may want to reference any functional specifications, test plans, customer problem reports, or any other data that are useful for other individuals who may need to review your changes.

2 Next, check out your C program (**myfile.c**) with a lock.

3 Now, check and make sure that no one else (including yourself) is able to check out the file with a lock.

4 What command displays comments that were provided during check in for all RCS files in the current working directory?

9.5   LIBRARIES AND THE APPLICATION BINARY INTERFACE (ABI)

As mentioned earlier, a **library** is a collection of object files that can be linked with a C program to create a binary executable file. Libraries are good because they provide and encourage source code reuse. For example, rather than having each programmer create a program to print data to the user's display, the UNIX system provides the **printf** function. This function is included in the standard C library and was used by our program **myfile.c** in the previous section. Having a standard library function rather than many individual functions provides many benefits, including reduced disk space, improved quality, reduced development and maintenance costs, and support.

The UNIX operating system provides the ability for binary programs to be executed or shared by different system vendors using the same microprocessor. The UNIX generic and processor-specific Application Binary Interface (ABI) standards define the requirements for libraries and binary files. The end result is that when a program such as **myfile.c** is compiled on one system, it can be successfully executed on another computer system using the same microprocessor. Binary portability has been a problem for UNIX for several years; however, it has been partially eliminated through the ABI standard. I said "partially" because the ABI only provides portable binaries for systems that use the same microprocessor. For example, a program compiled on one microprocessor is executable only on other systems that use the same microprocessor architecture. However, if an emulator is used, machine instructions for one microprocessor can be emulated on another. In fact, this has been demonstrated with the Windows NT operating system when a Microsoft application created using the Intel microprocessor was executed on a Mips processor computer system. (There are significant performance penalties whenever an instruction emulator is used.)

The major trick behind the UNIX ABI is that machine-specific kernel functions are included in a special type of library known as a *shared library*. A shared library is different from a *static library* or *archive library* in that it does not fully resolve all source code functional call references (e.g., **read**) during the link (**ld**) phase. (This method is also often called *lazy binding*.) This means that when the program is first executed, all functions that are used by the program are linked (resolved) by a special run-time loader, **rld**. Because the run-time loader waits until program execution to resolve machine-specific functions contained in the UNIX kernel, the program can wait to perform many tasks at the last minute via the run-time loader. Using this method, we can take a program compiled on one UNIX system and execute it on a different system and have binary portability (assuming both systems are binary-compatible and use the same microprocessor). The benefit is that different system vendors can have their own UNIX implementation (kernel, libraries, and commands) that may improve system performance and yet share in the benefits of having only one binary executable. This makes

application vendors much more happy because they do not have to create binary files for each and every UNIX system. (In 1980, one UNIX-language vendor reported that it had ported its application to over 400 different UNIX platforms.) Can you imagine trying to support 400 different versions of a product?

The command to create, delete, and add object files to a static archive (library) is **ar**. The best way to demonstrate the **ar** command is to first create our own private function foo and then add a function to our static library archive **lib-foo.a**. Finally, we link our program **myfile2.c** with our library to create a binary program. We must create our function in a C file called **foo.c** using the editor that contains the following:

```
foo()
{
/* This is a sample function to simply display "I'm function foo" */
printf ("I'm function foo \n");
return();
}
```

The characters between the /* and */ start and end a comment in C language. (In C++ language, you can use a // for a single line comment.) The **return** function returns control back to the calling program, in this case, **myfile2.c** (which contains the following):

```
main()
{
/* Call the function "foo" */
foo();
}
```

Now we must compile both programs; however, first, we must create our library archive (**libfoo.a**) so we can successfully compile our program.

In the following example, we first partially complete the compilation process by creating an object file for **foo.c** (**foo.o**):

```
% cc -c foo.c
% ar cr libfoo.a foo.o
% ar tv libfoo.a
rw-r--r--5616/12 176 Sep 6 17:02 1994 foo.o
% ranlib libfoo.a
```

The second **ar** command displays the contents of our library. The third command shows that we have successfully created the file **foo.o** because the library **libfoo.a** now contains our object file. The **ranlib** command creates a table of contents for our library (required by the link editor command **ld** on BSD-based systems).

Next, we need to compile our program **myfile2.c** and make sure to add our library **libfoo.a** to the command line, as follows:

```
% cc myfile2.c libfoo.a -o myfile2
% a.out
I'm function foo
```

Exercise 4

1. Create your own C function to display your name and call the function myname. Call the name of the C file **myname.c**. *Hint*: For the sake of simplicity, use the **system** function to make a call to the UNIX shell to get your **login** name.

2. Compile the program **myname.c** and create an object file.

3. Create a static library called **mylibrary.a** that contains the object file **myname.o**.

4. What command creates a table of contents for the new archive?

5. Will you need to run this command each time you create, delete, or update objects in the library?

6. Finally, create and compile a simple program called test1.c to call your **myname** function. Execute the program and verify that it correctly displays your **login** name.

chapter 10

Basic System Administration

*U*NIX system administrators who are able to deal with different flavors of UNIX (i.e., BSD, System V, and custom ports) will continue to be in great demand for many more years to come. The UNIX standardization effort has made great progress toward "unifying" the UNIX operating system; however, system administration remains one of the more challenging areas for consistency across UNIX systems. This challenge includes items such as device names, kernel construction, and reconfiguration, as well as printer administration and adding new accounts.

The purpose of this chapter is to expose the new UNIX user to the various commands used for system administration. Experienced system administrators should also find many new useful techniques for managing the care and feeding of your UNIX system.

The UNIX system administrator is responsible for the proper operation of all computing system resources, including hardware devices and peripherals. In this chapter, we discuss the following system administration tasks:

- The bootstrap process
- Selective backup and restore (**tar, cpio,** and **dd** commands)

116

- Adding, deleting, and modifying user accounts
- Printer configuration
- The disk usage and disk free commands
- Formatting and making file systems
- Mounting file systems
- File system maintenance
- Processes
- The **cron** and **at** programs
- Setting up **uucp**
- Quick network debugging and troubleshooting
- The Serial Line Internet Protocol (SL/IP)
- Configuration files for the X Window System
- The File Transfer Protocol (**ftp**)
- The **telnet** command

10.1 THE BOOTSTRAP PROCESS

The UNIX system must be loaded into physical memory for the operating system to be operational. This process is often called booting and comes from the expression "pulling yourself up by your bootstraps." The BSD version of UNIX provides two modes of booting the system, either single-user or multiuser. The single-user mode provides access only through the console display or terminal device. Therefore, only the system administrator usually has access to the operating system and computing resources (the console device is often located in a secure room). The single-user mode is often used by the system administrator for maintenance and repair activities. The single-user mode is required, for example, when a disk drive (file system) must be rebuilt and recovered from backup media (usually 4-mm or 8-mm tape). With the multiuser mode, other users can log in to UNIX using either serial- or ethernet-based communication interfaces (i.e., dumb terminals, PCs, or workstations).

The System V Release 4 version of UNIX provides several possible modes of operation other than just single and multiuser. The **init** program reads the **inittab** file located in the /etc directory to determine the default run-state level. For example, the system administrator may determine that only limited networking services will be provided by default during the boot process. The following run levels are commonly defined in the **/etc/inittab** file (level 4 is often the default run level and means that levels 1 through 3 already are complete):

- 0 Shutdown and power off
- 1 Single-user mode

- 2 Multiuser mode
- 3 Start NFS and mail daemons
- 4 Start xdm (X Display Manager)
- 5 Halt to Read Only Memory (ROM) monitor (boot prompt)
- 6 Reboot

To continue to multiuser mode from the single-user mode, the system administrator must enter a ^D (hold down the control and D keys together) at the single-user mode prompt. The **shutdown** command is commonly used to reboot the system. The **shutdown** command uses the **wall** command to write to all users. All users that are on the system are notified of a system shutdown and that they must log off the system immediately.

10.2 SELECTIVE BACKUP AND RESTORE

The tar Command

The **tar** command for tape archive creation and extraction is one of the most important commands provided with the UNIX operating system. This is because this command can be used to copy and create a backup copy of user files and directories. The **tar** command provides three primary operations: Create, eXtract, and Table of contents (**c**, **x**, **t**). The verbose **v** option is also useful for displaying details such as file permission, ownership, creation date and time, and name. You can create a **tar** archive on disk, tape, floppy, or any storage device. In the first example, we use the floppy device **/dev/rfd0** to create a backup of our files (make sure to format your floppy first using **format** or **fdformat**):

```
% tar cvf /dev/rfd0 .
a ./check_for_file 1 blocks
a ./RCS/myfile.c,v 1 blocks
a ./myfile.c 1 blocks
% tar tvf /dev/rfd0
```

drwxr-xr-x 5616/12	512	Sep 6 17:40 1994	./
-rwxr-xr-x 5616/12	144	Sep 9 17:45 1994	./checkf
drwxr-xr-x 5616/12	512	Sep 6 15:30 1994	./RCS/
-r--r--r-- 5616/12	299	Sep 6 15:24 1994	./RCS/a.c,v
-rw-r--r-- 5616/12	136	Sep 6 15:24 1994	./myfile.c

The second command displays the table of contents (listing of files) for the floppy disk **tar** archive. It is important to notice that each file on the floppy disk starts with a ".*/*". This is used to designate that the file has been created using a *relative path*. Using the relative path method of backup with **tar**, we can extract files from the **tar** archive to any other directory location. However, if we had specified the complete or *absolute path*, we could only extract files from the **tar** archive to the designated path location. For example, let us copy the **passwd** file to a hard disk **tar** archive file called **mybackup** using the **tar** command:

> % **tar cvf mybackup /etc/passwd**
> % **tar tvf mybackup**
> rw-r--r-- 0/10 299 Sep 6 15:24 1994 /etc/passwd

Because the file has been created using the complete or absolute path, the file **passwd** only can be copied back to its original location (the **/etc** directory). In some cases, absolute path names are desired, especially during software installation. However, in many cases, absolute paths are not helpful (e.g., often you will want to store the backup files in a new directory location). The key to creating **tar** archives with relative paths is to remember to use the "." character. The "dot" ensures that the current working directory and all subdirectories are used. Now, let us remove the file **myfile.c** and extract the backup copy from our **tar** archive on floppy:

> % **rm myfile.c**
> % **ls myfile.c**
> % **tar xvf /dev/rfd0 ./myfile.c**
> **x** ./myfile.c, 36 bytes, 1 tape blocks
> % **ls -l myfile.c**
> -rw-r--r-- 1 rodney 36 Sep 6 15:24 myfile.c

It is also important to notice that when you extract files from a **tar** archive, the user name with which you are currently logged in, will become the owner of the files as they are extracted. To avoid this problem, some versions of **tar** provide a command -**P** line option to preserve file ownership as defined in the original **tar** archive. Alternatively, on most systems, when the superuser extracts files from a **tar** archive, the original ownership and permission are preserved. (See Exercise 1.)

The cpio Command

The **cpio** command provides facilities similar to **tar** for copying files in and out of backup archives. The **cpio** command is provided with most System V—based UNIX systems, whereas the **tar** command comes standard with most BSD systems. System V Release 4 (SVR4) provides several commands for software installation and maintenance that are based upon **cpio**. SVR4 commands for

Exercise 1

1 Use the **tar** command to create a copy of the files in your home directory on a floppy disk or tape device. Use the **du -s** command to determine the total amount of disk space consumed by your home directory. If the total size is greater than 1 MB, it is suggested that you use a tape device for backup.

2 Alternatively, if you do not have floppy devices, create a **tar** archive on your hard disk called **mybackup.tar**.

3 What command lists the contents of your **tar** archive?

4 Use the **mv** command to move a file in your current working directory to a new name (e.g., **dummy**).

5 Use the **tar** command to extract the file you just moved to **dummy**.

6 What commands can you use to compare the two files (i.e., the file that you extracted from your **tar** archive with the file called **dummy**)?

7 Use one of these commands to verify that the backup copy is identical to the original (i.e., moved file).

---

package installation, deleting, checking, and information include **pkgadd, pkgdel, pkgchk,** and **pkginfo,** respectively. To copy all files in your current working directory to the floppy disk in **cpio** format, use the following command:

```
% find . -depth -print | cpio -o > /dev/rfd0
2 blocks
```

Because we do not have very much data in our current working directory, the entire **cpio** copy only consumed two disk blocks, or 1024 bytes or characters (BSD systems). The **find** command is used instead of the **ls** command because we want to make sure to collect all files contained in all subdirectories (i.e., the **-depth** option provides this ability). Now we can create a new directory called

copydir and copy all directories and files from the floppy and compare the copy with our original tree:

```
% cd copydir
% cpio -icd < /dev/rfd0
2 blocks
```

You can use the **-R** option to the **ls** command for a recursive listing for both source and destination directories and compare the results of the **cpio** operations.

Exercise 2

1 Use the **cpio** command to create a backup of your current working directory to floppy disk or tape. If you are not sure what devices you have connected to your system, use the **prtconf** (SVR4) or the **dmesg** (BSD) commands. Again, it is recommended that if you have consumed over 1 MB of hard disk space that you to use a tape device for backup. Use the **du** command to determine your total disk usage if you are not sure how much space has been consumed.

The dd Command

The **dd** command is used for disk-to-disk copy. This command, unlike **tar** and **cpio**, does not create an archive file in a special format for backup and recovery. However, it does provide fast copying of raw data from one file to another. This is one method of creating an exact copy of a disk for backup and recovery. This process is also known as a *hot backup*, or *disk mirroring*, because the data copy is quick and efficient. Having access to a hot backup can often mean the difference between just rebooting the system with a different disk and having to reinstall the entire operating system from scratch.

The following commands first display the device names for the **root** and **usr** file systems and create a duplicate copy of the **root** partition on a second disk drive. This operation should be performed in case of emergency. (You need to be the superuser to perform these operations. It is also recommended that both file systems be unmounted. Therefore, you want to use a secondary disk drive as your source disk.)

```
% mount
/dev/sd0a on / type 4.2 (rw)
/dev/sd0g on /usr type 4.2 (rw)
```

% dd if=/dev/sd0a of=/dev/sd1a
46740+0 records in
46740+0 records out

The physical device **/dev/sd0a** is the source disk for the root file system and **/dev/sd1a** is the backup hard disk device (BSD systems). These devices are known as *block devices* because they contain the UNIX file system information as well as files and directories. The map information contained in the file system is also known as the *superblock*. Each disk device should be partitioned with the same size physical partitions before using the **dd** command to create an exact copy for backup. The requirement is that the destination disk must be equal to or larger than the source. If the destination disk is larger, it simply means that there will be disk blocks that will never be used. This operation must be performed when both file systems are unmounted (use the **umount** command as superuser).

Check the UNIX on-line manual page for **format** (BSD systems) and **fmthard** (System V systems) for details about creating identical physical partitions for both disks. The root physical device required 46,740 blocks during the copy. You can also improve performance of the **dd** copy by increasing the default block size to something larger than 512 bytes. For example, add **bs=2048** to the end of the preceding **dd** commands to make the block sizes used for copying four times as large as the default.

Another useful application of the **dd** command is to create a large scratch file for increasing system *swap space*. The UNIX operating system used a special area located on the disk called swap for *virtual-memory* operations. Virtual memory allows user processes to believe that they actually have more physical memory than is physically available during program execution. Using a method called *paging*, the UNIX kernel moves pieces or pages (512 bytes) of memory from the swap area on the disk (**pagein**) to physical memory. Later, this same page of memory may be sent back to disk again (**pageout**). A *physical page* is usually always 512 bytes; however, *logical pages* can be much larger. A logical page is the amount of data the UNIX kernel uses for paging operations.

UNIX System V Release 4 provides the ability to swap from a regular file as well as a UNIX file system. The **dd** command can be used to create a large scratch file that later can be used to increase system swap space. The following command creates a slightly less than 5 megabyte[*] file called **swapfile** using the **count** option of the **dd** command. This file (**swapfile**) can then be used to increase swap space using the **swap** command with System V Release 4— based systems:

% dd if=/dev/sd0a of=/tmp/swapfile count=10000
10000+0 records in
10000+0 records out

---

[*]5 megabytes is actually 5*1024*1024, which is 5,242,880. This is 10000*512, which is only 5,120,000.

To verify the size of the file **swapfile**, we can use the **ls** command with the long listing option, as follows:

% **ls -l swapfile**
-rw-r--r-- 1 root 5120000 Sep 7 09:46 swapfile

Exercise 3

1 Use the **dd** command to create a file called **empty_file** that is 512 bytes in size.

2 What commands can you use to verify the file size?

3 The **dd** command can also be used to swap data bytes within a file. This is often useful when data must be copied from one system to another with an incompatible byte ordering. Use the **conv=swab** option of the **dd** command to view the contents of the **mypasswd** file with bytes that have been swapped.

10.3   ADDING, DELETING, AND MODIFYING USER ACCOUNTS

Because UNIX is a multiuser system, each user must have a unique account name for **login**. This account name restricts access to files and directories. System V versions of UNIX also provide additional security features that often require users to change their passwords after a specified period of time. It is the system administrator's responsibility to manage user accounts. This includes adding, deleting, and modifying user accounts and groups.

One of the greatest dangers in account management is the possible damage to the root or system administration account. For example, if the encrypted password string for root contained in the **/etc/passwd** file is corrupted during editing and the root user exits the system, no one will be able to log into the system as the root again. This is a critical problem because no user can log in and perform system **shutdown** or other common system administration functions. The System V Release 4 version of UNIX provides the following commands for account management: **useradd**, **userdel**, and **usermod**.

The following command adds user "joe" with user id 99 as a member of group 292. This user's home is **/home/joe** and uses the C shell as the default log in shell:

% **useradd -u 99 -g 292 -d/home/joe -s/bin/csh joe**

Using a command interface for account management instead of editing the file is safer and prevents many potential accidents. User accounts can also be modified and deleted in this same way. Group information contained in the **/etc/group** file can also be added, deleted, or modified using the **groupadd**, **groupdel**, and **groupmod** commands respectively.

Exercise 4

1 Log in to the system as the system administrator and create an account for yourself. Call this account **test** and give the **test** user a default shell of **/bin/csh**.

2 Another useful account to create is for the automatic correction of line printer errors. For example, create an account called **printer**.

3 Now, create a shell script that is executed by this account to **restart** the line printer daemon using the **lpc** command (BSD systems). Make sure to include an **exit** statement as the last command in the shell script as you do not want to jeopardize security. It is important to include a trap handler in the **printer** shell script that prevents users from escaping out of the script to a shell prompt.

4 The shell script has to be executed using the root user log in shell instead of a standard shell. Therefore, the *set uid bit* must also be set on the file permission mask for the shell script so that the user **printer** has root permission. What command sets the permissions in this manner?

10.4 PRINTER CONFIGURATION

Adding printers with UNIX System V—based systems is somewhat more difficult than with BSD systems. However, the following five commands provide the core functions for printer administration and setup:

- **lpsystem** (printer system registration: remote printing)
- **lpadmin** (printer administration: configure print services)
- **accept** (printer acceptance of print requests)
- **enable** (printer is enabled to start printing)
- **lpstat** (status information for print queue)

Because printers are often expensive, it is useful to have many systems share a single high-speed printer. One of the major benefits of the UNIX operating system is the many available networking protocols and facilities provided. The **lpsystem** command allows users to register their system with a remote system as a local printer. The next command, **lpadmin**, allows the system administrator to configure printing to a remote or local system printer. Finally, the **accept** and **enable** commands allow spooling of print requests and actual printing to occur.

With a System V Release 4 UNIX system, we can issue the following command to register a printer system name **remote1** for a remote printer on a BSD UNIX system:

% **lpsystem -t bsd remote1**

The following command configures the **remote1** system printer (**lp**) as our local printer with the name **lp**:

% **lpadmin -p lp -s remote1\!lp**

Notice that the exclamation point is escaped using the "\" character. This also tells the **lpadmin** command that we want to use the **lp** printer on the remote system for printing when we use our local printer **lp**. Now we need to allow the printer to accept our print requests, so we use the **accept** command, as follows:

% **accept lp**

Finally, we must **enable** the printer to start printing:

% **enable lp**

To make the remote printer **lp** (now also our local **lp** printer, the default printer, we use the **lpadmin** command with the **-d** option:

% lpadmin -d lp

Now, to print the file **myfile.c** on the **remote1** printer system's **lp** printer, type the following:

% lp myfile.c

To obtain status information, use the **lpstat** command, as follows:

```
% lpstat -t -L
lp:
Wed Sep 7 10:40:24 1994
 Job in progress--- Status: IDLE
Rank       Owner Job      Files          Total Size
active     rodney 477     myfile.c       10 bytes
```

The **cancel** command removes an active print job from the spooler (printer's queue). You must provide the job number and the name of the printer. The following command removes job 477 from the printer **lp** (you must be the owner of the job or root to perform this function and on a BSD system):

% cancel 477 lp

The following command is used to **reject** all print requests for the **lp1** printer because it is currently being serviced:

% reject -r "Printer is currently being serviced" lp1

The **lpmove** command then can be used to reassign all existing print requests from the **lp1** printer to the **lp2** printer, as follows:

% lpmove lp1 lp2

The following BSD commands also can be used for printing and printer adminstration: **lpr, lpq,** and **lprm.** To print a file on the printer using the BSD program type, the following:

% lpr myfile.c

To check the status of the print spooler (i.e., all the current requests that are in the queue) on a BSD system, type the following:

```
% lpq
Rank      Owner       Job    Files          Total Size
1st       rodney      18     dead.letter    96 bytes
```

If you determine that you want to remove your request, identify the request number from the **lpq** command and execute the **lprm** command, as follows:

```
% lprm 18
```

Exercise 5

1 What command allows you to print the file **myfile.c** on the line printer when using a BSD system?

2 What if we wanted to print **myfile.c** on a System V system?

3 What commands allow you to check the status of all print jobs in the queue for a BSD system? How about for a System V system?

4 What command removes a current active print request from the print spooler?

5 What command allows the system administrator to stop all print requests for the printer **lp** and inform all users that the printer is currently unavailable?

10.5 THE DISK USAGE AND DISK FREE COMMANDS

The hard disk drive is one of the most precious hardware resources next to physical memory and the central microprocessor unit. Many people consider that everything in UNIX is really just a file. For example, each device must have an associated device file name for the kernel to provide the necessary services such as reading and writing.* Because the availability of the disk device is so important, it is critical that the amount of disk space available on the hard disk be carefully monitored by the system administrator. The disk usage command, **du**, is used to provide information on a file-by-file basis. The following command

---

*All UNIX device files are located in the **/dev** directory.

(**du,** short for disk usage) provides a summary (via the **-s** option) of disk blocks consumed for each file in the current working directory:

```
% du -s *
27061      ADI
180        BBL
8          BESTBREED
13         BETA
4659       CLASSES
```

The size of a disk block varies, depending on the version of UNIX that is used. Most System V versions of UNIX use 512-byte blocks. BSD versions of UNIX use kilobyte (1024-byte) blocks to represent the amount of disk used. In the preceding example, directory **BESTBREED** is consuming approximately 8000 bytes or characters of information for a BSD-UNIX system.

The disk free command, **df,** is used to provide information on a file system by file system basis. The system administrator uses this command to determine if a complete file system may be in danger of running out of disk space. The results of the **df** command are similar to the **mount** command because both commands provide data for each mounted file system, including NFS mounted files systems (i.e., disks located on remote systems connected via ethernet):

```
% df
```

Filesystem	kbytes	used	avail	capacity	Mounted on
/dev/sd0a	21865	7091	12588	36%	/
/dev/sd0g	1786130	1412024	195493	88%	/usr
/dev/sd1c	189858	146304	24569	86%	/usr1
mysys:/	15487	5386	8553	39%	/net/mysys
bigsys:/usr	279039	168809	82327	67%	/net/bigsys/usr

Exercise 6

1 Use the disk usage command to determine which users on your system are using the majority of disk space.

2 Identify the file systems on your system that will run out of disk space first.

3 What are some potential remedies that you can think of to increase the available space for these file systems?

10.6   MOUNTING FILE SYSTEMS

A file system contains the structure, or map, for all files and directories contained within a physical partition located on the hard disk drive. File systems cannot overlap physical disk partitions, for example, if partition **a** is from 0 to 100 and partition **b** is from 20 to 1000. Both partitions **a** and **b** can be used (i.e., they can create a file system for each partition and mount each file system for user access).

Each file system must be mounted in order to allow users access to the files and directories contained in the file system structure (superblock or disk map). All file systems must be mounted under the **root** file system. This file system is also defined as "/". Both the physical device name and a mount point must be provided to the **mount** command, as follows:

> % **mount /dev/fd0/fd /floppy**

This command mounts the floppy disk to a directory called **/floppy**. The previous contents of the directory **/floppy** no longer are available until the **umount** command is used, as follows:

> % **umount /floppy**

The previous contents of the directory **/floppy** are not available once again, because we now have unmounted the floppy disk. Mounting a file system on top of an existing directory structure does not disturb the contents of the existing directory. See the next section on formatting and making file systems and for Exercise 7 dealing with mounting file systems.

10.7   FORMATTING AND MAKING FILE SYSTEMS

In order to mount a floppy disk as a file system, you must first **format** and create a file system on the floppy disk itself. To accomplish this, you can use the **format** or **fdformat** (SunOS systems) command.

Next, the **newfs** or **mkfs** command is used to create a file system on the formatted media (i.e., floppy disk device). The **newfs** command consults a **disktab** file located in the **/etc** directory. The **newfs** command eliminates the need to provide disk geometry information, as is the case with the **mkfs** command. (Disk geometry information often includes the total number cylinders per track, sectors per track and other physical constraints of the disk drive.) You need to make sure to specify the raw floppy disk device and not the block device when creating a file

system. The block device then is required for mounting the file system along with a mount point after the file system has been successfully created.

See the on-line man page for the floppy device on your system for more instructions on floppy disk naming conventions, as this varies from system to system. In order to gain access to the files on the floppy or hard disk device, you must first **mount** the device to a mount point (directory in the root file system). See the previous section for details regarding the **mount** command. The **fsck** command also can be used to clean and repair a damaged file system. See the next section for more details concerning the **fsck** command.

Most floppies can be formatted as either 720 KB or 1440 KB (kilobytes or 1024 bytes). Many systems provide the **eject** command to automatically discard the floppy disk from the drive. Note, you and any other users must not be located in the directory where the file system was mounted during the **umount** command. For example, to properly **umount** a floppy disk device, you must change directories to somewhere other than the **/floppy** directory hierarchy (if that is where the floppy was mounted).

The **volcheck** command also can be used by non root users to mount MS-DOS formatted floppies. If your floppy does not have a volume label, the directory **noname** will be created under the **/floppy** directory after the **volcheck** command is executed.

Exercise 7

1 Insert a floppy disk into your floppy disk drive (make sure that it does not contain a write protect tab over the cut out notch). Format the floppy disk you have just inserted using either low (720 KB) or high (1440 KB) density.

2 Finally, issue the command to create a UNIX file system on the floppy disk that you just formatted.

3 Now, create a directory under the root file system on your hard disk called **floppy** and mount the floppy disk to the **/floppy** directory (you need to be the root to accomplish both operations).

4 Copy all C program source files (e.g., **myfile.c**) to the floppy disk.

5 Unmount the floppy once you are finished (you also need to be the root).

6 What command can you use to mount an MS-DOS formatted floppy?

10.8   FILE SYSTEM MAINTENANCE

It is the system administrator who is responsible for managing the file system by making sure that adequate free space is available for all users. The system administrator is also responsible for ensuring that the hard disk is not fragmented, as well as performing other engineering tasks. *Fragmentation* occurs when many small disk files (blocks) are located throughout the disk, making it difficult for one or more large files to allocate several sequential disk blocks. One method that can be used to eliminate the problem of disk fragmentation is to back up the disk using an image backup utility (e.g., **ufsdump** or **dump**). Next, once the backup has been verified, the disk can be formatted and a new file system created. Finally, the backup archive can be restored to the new file system.

One method that is commonly used to maintain sufficient free space on the hard disk is to inform users using the **wall** command or **motd** (Message Of The Day) file that there is a disk free space shortage. Unfortunately, this often is unsuccessful as most users are too busy to evaluate what files could be eliminated. Therefore, a better approach is just to prune away old dead files. This can be accomplished using the **find** command with the modification time (**mtime**) option (see previous chapters). It also useful to search and eliminate old **core** files that have been created as a result of a memory-access violation (reading or writing to a memory location that is not owned by the current process). The **quotaon** and **quotaoff** (BSD UNIX) commands can be used to set a **quota** on the maximum amount of disk space (per file system) that can be consumed by each user. The **quota** command is useful for displaying disk usage and limits by the user. Only the superuser (root) can identify user **quotas** by name; other users can see only their disk quota status.

The **fsck** (file system check) command also can be used by the system administrator to check the file system. This command reads information located in the superblock (file system map) to determine if all disk blocks (books) are in order. Remember, the UNIX operating system is like an accountant that is responsible for making sure that all transactions or operations are performed successfully. The **fsck** command reads the contents of the superblock to determine if the file system needs repair. If the superblock is corrupted, by using the BSD fast file system (also available with the System V Release 4 version of UNIX), alternate superblocks can be specified using the -b option of **fsck**. The **fsck** command is executed as part of the boot process whenever a file system's *dirty bit* has been set. For example, if the disk drive has a hardware problem (head crash) or the system power is suddenly turned off, the file system integrity must always be questioned (the dirty bit is set). As a result of both failures, the **fsck** command is executed as part of the boot process. Performing an orderly **shutdown** helps eliminate the potential need for a file system check during reboot. The **fastboot** command (BSD

systems) also can be used to reboot the system and to avoid the need for a file system check (**fsck**) during the boot process if the dirty bit has not been set. The UNIX operating system marks a file system as dirty if any number of potential events occur (e.g., a system crash during a power failure).

Exercise 8

1 Create a shell script that searches the entire UNIX file system hierarchy for **core** files that are over 30 days old.

2 Add to this script the ability to warn all users that a **core** file will be removed in 2 weeks. What other files may be good candidates for removal?

10.9   PROCESSES

A process may sometimes need to be terminated prior to completion. The **kill** command can be used to accomplish this requirement. The process status (**ps**) command can be used to identify the process id. Once the process id, or pid, has been identified, the **kill** command can be executed, as follows:

    % kill 1234

The **kill** command also accepts a signal number as an option. The following example uses the "sure kill" or **SIGKILL** signal as defined in the **/usr/include/sys/signal.h** file:

    % kill -9 1234

This method is especially useful for programs that have been written to ignore the **kill** signal during program termination. It is always best not to use the "sure kill", or -9 option, because the program will not be given the opportunity to clean up prior to termination. Many programs often have trap or exception handlers that are executed prior to program termination. If the -9 option is used with the **kill** command, these routines will be bypassed during termination. Many difficulties often arise as a result of not allowing a program to terminate properly. For example, a database record or a temporary file may be corrupted as a result of improper program termination. Do not get into the bad habit of always using the

-9 option with the **kill** command. Note, you need to be the owner of the process to use the **kill** command successfully (i.e., you must have started the program). The system administrator (root) does not have to be the owner of a process to use the **kill** command successfully.

Exercise 9

1 Provide an example of creating a sub shell process.

2 What command terminates the child shell process?

3 What command can you use to determine your current shell process id (just processes that you have created)?

4 Perform the same task, however, this time use a shell script that is defined to ignore the termination signal.

5 How can you kill this process?

10.10 THE CRON AND AT PROGRAMS

The **cron** program is usually started automatically during system boot. The purpose of **cron** is to read the **cron** table, or **crontab** file, on a periodic basis. The **crontab** file contains programs that are defined to execute at specific times. The system administrator often relies upon the **cron** program to schedule backups and other operations that are best conducted during nonbusiness hours (i.e., early hours in the morning). The system administrator can also specify users that will not be able to create a **crontab** file or **at** job by specifying the user's names in the **cron.deny** and **at.deny** files. Alternatively, if the **cron.allow** or **at.allow** files contain any names, then only those users will be allowed to use the **cron** and **at** commands. The **at** command is similar to the **cron** function; however, the **at** command reads instructions directly from the command line instead of a file. For example, to execute the **atscript** command shell script at 10:15 A.M., enter the following command (you will usually want to redirect any output or errors to a file):

% **at 10:15 /rodney/atscript**
job 5874 at Fri Dec 9 10:15:00 1994

The **crontab** can be modified using the **vi** editor after specifying the **-e** option to **crontab**. The **crontab** file can be listed using the **-l** option. The following example shows a **crontab** file that backs up Rodney Wilson's home directory to a remote server called **system1** at 11:30 P.M. each night:

% **crontab -l**
#Comment: Backup Rodney Wilson's home directory nightly.
30 23 * * * /usr/ucb/rcp -r /rodney system1:/rodney > /tmp/log 2>&1

The first field, "30", is the minutes past the hour. The second field is the hour (in military time, 0–23). The third field is the calendar day of the month. The fourth field is the month of the year (1–12). The fifth field is the day of the week (0–6, where Sunday is always 0). The sixth, or last, field is the command to execute. It is strongly suggested that the output and error message of the command line that are to be executed be redirected to a log file. This is because when **cron** executes the commands in the **crontab** file, no output device is assigned for output and error messages.

Exercise 10

1　Create an example **crontab** file to back up your home directory from Monday through Friday, each night at 2 A.M.

2　Update your **crontab** entry so that it displays all errors and output to a file in your home directory called **backup_errors**. Why is this important?

10.11 SETTING UP UUCP

The UNIX-to-UNIX copy (**uucp**) program provides many networking facilities. Its roots go back before the information superhighway (the Internet) when modems were the standard device for communications between computer systems. The HoneyDanBer (HDB) version of **uucp** is the most commonly used package and is provided with UNIX System V Release 4. (This version was named after its authors: Peter Honeyman, David A. Nowitz, and Brian E. Redman.) There are several files associated with the setup and administration of **uucp**.

These files include the following:

- **Config**
- **Devconfig**
- **Devices**
- **Dialcodes**
- **Dialers**
- **Grades**
- **Limits**
- **Permissions**
- **Poll**
- **Sysfiles**
- **Systems**

The **Devices** file is the first file that should be created. It includes five fields, defined as follows:

rodney ttys0 - 9600 direct

- Field 1, "rodney", contains the name or label you will use in the **Systems** file.
- Field 2, "ttys0", is the name of the physical port you will use to connect to the other system (if you are using a null modem for the direct connect method). Alternatively, this device can be the physical port with a modem connected for remote communications. In both cases, this port on the system is usually a serial port that contains a standard RS-232 interface, in other words, a connector that can accept a 25-pin connector. The RS-232 EIA interface defines the purpose of each pin.
- Field 3, "-", contains the name or label and is generally not used.
- Field 4, "9600", defines the speed (baud or bits per second) to use. If the keyword "Any" is specified, the speed will be determined from the **Systems** file.
- Field 5, "direct", defines the dialer label (defined in the **Dialers** file). This important field defines how the modem is to be dialed and often contains what is called a "chat" script, for example, how long to wait after the remote modem picks up the phone before sending any data.

After the **Devices** file has been configured, the **Systems** file must be edited. This file includes six fields for definition of remote systems for **uucp** communication. The following example is for a remote system called "rodney1":

rodney1 Any rodney 9600 - in:--in: rodney1 word: LetMeIn

- Field 1, "rodney1", is the name of the remote system you want to call.
- Field 2, "Any", is the time when it is ok to call. (In this case, any time is fine.)
- Field 3, "rodney", contains the device label to use (from the **Devices** file).
- Field 4, "9600", contains the speed with which to connect to that system (9600 baud in this case).
- Field 5, "-", contains the phone number to dial. In this case, no number is specified for the remote system "rodney1".
- Field 6, "in:--in: rodney1 word: LetMeIn", contains the expected send sequence to use for **login** to the remote system "rodney1".

The next step is to make sure that an account exists for the user "rodney1" on the remote system "rodney1". The **Permissions** file must also be set up on the remote system "rodney1". If you want to give the user "rodney1" the ability to read and write files in the **/usr/uucp/uucppublic** directory, request and send files, and **mail** and **uucp** files, add the following to the **Permissions** file:

```
LOGNAME=rodney1 MACHINE=rodney1 \
READ=/usr/spool/uucppublic WRITE=/usr/spool/uucppublic \
REQUEST=yes SENDFILES=yes \
COMMANDS=/usr/bin/mail /usr/bin/uucp
```

The remote system "rodney1" also must have a **getty** (BSD systems) or a **ttymod** (SVR4 systems) process running on the modem port, so that the local system's modem can connect successfully, **login**, and initiate a copy operation (e.g., **mail** transfer). After configuration of the preceding files, the user can use the **cu** command to "call UNIX" and test the proper setup and configuration of **uucp**. The syntax of **cu** can include either a physical device port (after the **-l** option) or a system name to call. The following example calls the UNIX system "rodney1" to test the proper configuration of the **Devices** and **Systems** files:

```
% cu rodney1
```

10.12 QUICK NETWORK DEBUGGING AND TROUBLESHOOTING

There are several commands that are provided to help troubleshoot networking problems. The **ping** command attempts to send network packets to a remote hosts and verify that a specific system can be reached using the network hardware and software as configured. If the remote host is not defined, the following type of message may be returned:

> % **ping nobody**
> ping: unknown host nobody

If the remote host that is specified after the **ping** command is available and operational, a message will be returned from **ping** that states that the system is alive. The **ping** command is useful as an initial step in troubleshooting network communications problems. It is also important to remember to check the **/etc/hosts** file to determine if the remote host name and Internet Protocol (IP) number is correctly defined.

The **arp** command can be used to determine the Internet (logical address) to physical address translation. Each computer system's ethernet interface has a unique hexadecimal number that is usually burned into a Read Only Memory (ROM) chip. If the **ping** utility is able to successfully communicate with a remote host, the **arp** table will be updated to reflect both the Internet and physical ethernet address of the remote host. For example:

> % **ping bigsystem**
> bigsystem is alive
>
> % **arp -a**
> bigsystem (148.150.40.18) at 8:0:20:d:2b:81

It is also important to check the physical network connection on the local and remote host (if possible) if the **ping** command is unable to connect to a remote host. The **ifconfig** command determines if the physical ethernet interface is up and operational (accepted and transmitting network packets). Marking the ethernet interface as operational is usually performed automatically during the boot process by the **ifconfig** program. The **netstat -i** command also can be used to determine if all available ethernet interfaces are currently configured and available.

10.13 THE SERIAL LINE INTERNET PROTOCOL (SL/IP)

The Serial Line Internet Protocol (SL/IP) provides an important capability for users who desire to work from home; however, who need network access to remote facilities. Using a modem from home, a user can connect to a remote system that is attached to a network. The modem connection using SL/IP looks virtually as if the user were connected using an ethernet interface instead of a serial

modem over a standard telephone line. In other words, SL/IP provides ethernet like multichannel capabilities instead of single-channel. The **uucp** protocol, for example, is single-channel and therefore only one session at a time is possible (e.g., file copy, **login**). With SL/IP, the user can have multiple sessions. Setup and configuration of SL/IP can be complicated; the following example shows the basic process:

```
% slattach -c on system2
% slattach -c on -d sl0 -l host1 host2
% sldetach system2
% sldetach host2
```

The first example connects to the remote system "system2" with character compression on. The second example uses the physical device **sl0**. For details regarding the fields in the **Systems** file, see the previous section on setting up and configuring **uucp**. The **/etc/uucp/Systems** file may contain data similar to the following, which is used to define the system called "system2":

```
system2 Any ACU 9600 1222 3333 "" \r in:--in:slip word:passwd
```

The **/etc/uucp/Devices** file also must be configured for proper operation of SL/IP. The following example defines an Automatic Call Unit (ACU) for the **sl0** port (as required by the **Systems** file entry):

```
ACU sl0 -9600 hayes \D
```

On the remote machine (system2), a password entry must be provided in the **/etc/passwd** file, as follows (i.e., assuming a SVR4 system in this case):

```
slip:x:999:900:slip:/home/slip:/usr/sbin/slreattach
```

Notice that the password entry for the SL/IP account does not execute a standard UNIX shell; instead, a special program called **slreattach** is provided. The contents of the file **/usr/sbin/slreattach** should contain the following:

```
/usr/sbin/slattach -
```

Finally, the remote system must have a **getty** (BSD) or **ttymon** (SVR4) process running on the modem port that we use to dial in (i.e., the receiving modem port). The local system must not have a **getty** or **ttymon**, as this would prevent us from successfully dialing out from the local host. Again, as is the case with **uucp**, it is strongly suggested that you test the proper configuration of the

Devices and **Systems** files by using the **cu** (call UNIX) command to connect to the remote system (i.e., system2). If you want to test the SL/IP interface using a modem and you have a local ethernet interface already configured, it is recommended that you first mark the ethernet interface "down" using the **ifconfig** command. (You need to be the root user to perform this command.) Afterward, you should be able to connect to the remote host using SL/IP.

10.14 INTRODUCTION TO THE X WINDOW SYSTEM AND XHOST AUTHORIZATION

The X Window System is a protocol that not only provides a graphical interface to the UNIX operating system, but also network communications using a client–server architecture. A client program often requires services provided by the X server. The X server provides many services for either local or remote clients, similar to the way the UNIX kernel is required for user commands. For example, the display device may be protected using the **xhost** command. Therefore, other systems are not allowed to send client program output, because they are considered to be unauthorized clients. To allow another system (client program) to send data, the local system must grant access using the **xhost** command. This special command notifies the X server that the display device can be shared across the network.

The following first example grants access to the local display and only to the host renegade. The second example grants access to all systems because the plus character is used (no specific host is identified). The third command removes access from the host renegade. The last command removes authorization from all systems:

% **xhost +renegade**
renegade being added to access control list

% **xhost +**
access control disabled, clients can connect from any host

% **xhost -renegade**
renegade being removed from access control list

% **xhost -**
access control enabled, only authorized clients can connect

The following block diagram shows the hierarchy, starting with the hardware all the way to a Graphical User Interface (GUI)–based application:

```
                              ┌─────────────────────┐
                              │ Application Program │
                         ┌────┴─────────────────────┤
                         │    Window Manager        │
              ┌──────────┼──────────────────────────┤
              │ Dumb TTY │    X Window System       │
              ├──────────┴──────────────────────────┤
              │      Operating System — UNIX         │
              ├──────────────────────────────────────┤
              │            Hardware                  │
              └──────────────────────────────────────┘
```

This block diagram shows the hierarchy of the operating system, X Window System, and Window Manager. The Motif Window Manager (**mwm**) from OSF has been determined to be the standard Window Manager for UNIX as a result of the Common Open Systems Environment (COSE) UNIX standardization effort. The Motif Window Manager looks very much like Microsoft Windows. Systems that do not have a *frame buffer* (display controller hardware and associated software drivers) are not able to use the X Window System. These systems use what is called a dumb terminal. A *dumb* terminal display is typically only 24 rows tall by 80 columns wide and therefore limits the amount of text that can be displayed. Dumb terminals also do not provide the ability to perform pixel operations (graphics primitives such as circles or other polygons cannot be rendered because the smallest addressable entity is character instead of a dot or pixel). Control operations using a mouse also are not possible using a dump terminal.

The X Window System uses **.xinitrc** or **.xsession** as a startup file to help determine what programs should be invoked during startup. The following **.xinitrc** file logs any errors in a file called **.xlog** (in the current working directory); for debugging, start the Motif Window Manager, followed by an **xclock**:

```
#!/bin/sh
exec > .xlog 2>&1
mwm &
xclock &
```

The **.mwmrc** file is used to define the popup windows that can be accessed using various mouse buttons. For example, the following **.mwmrc** file defines one choice (create a new window) when the first (right) mouse button is depressed:

```
Menu RightMouse
{
"Basic Operations"    f.title
"New Window"          f.exec "xterm &"
}
```

Another important startup file that is used for setup is **.Xdefaults**. This file is used by various X Window System client programs. For example, the **xterm** program is used to create an X terminal emulator. Each time the **xterm** program is started, the following resource definitions are used, as defined by the **.Xdefaults** file (located in the user's home directory):

```
! Here are some defaults for the xterm
xterm*foreground:     yellow
xterm*background:     darkslategrey
xterm*border:         turquoise
xterm*cursorColor:    yellow
xterm*scrollBar:      True
xterm*saveLines:      120
xterm*font:           9x15
```

In this example, the first line is a comment because it starts with an exclamation point. The second line defines the foreground color that is used for text characters inside the **xterm**. All input and output are in green. The background for the **xterm** is darkslategrey. The border around the window is turquoise and the cursor is yellow. A 120-line scroll bar is also provided (can view the previous 120 commands that have been executed). The next line defines the text size as 9 by 15 pixels. (A pixel is the smallest addressable unit on the display and is the size of a very small dot.) There are many other resources available for defining the characteristics of the X Window System environment. Each resource can be modified by the user; however, systemwide defaults are always provided.

10.15 THE FILE TRANSFER PROTOCOL (FTP)

The File Transfer Protocol (**ftp**) program is used to copy files from one host to another. The command can be used to copy files from or to a machine across the street or across the world. The following example shows how to copy the PERL archive from a remote host called **jpl-devvax.jpl.nasa.gov**:

```
% ftp jpl-devvax.jpl.nasa.gov
Connected to jpl-devvax.jpl.nasa.gov.
220 devvax FTP server (SunOS 4.1) ready.
```

Name (jpl-devvax.jpl.nasa.gov:rodney): **anonymous**
331 Guest login ok, send your complete e-mail address as password.
Password:
230 Guest login ok, access restrictions apply.

ftp> **cd pub**
250 CWD command successful.

ftp> **cd perl.4.0**
250 CWD command successful.

ftp> **cd kits@36**
250 CWD command successful.

ftp> **binary**
200 Type set to I.

ftp> **ls**
200 PORT command successful.
150 Opening ASCII mode data connection for file list.
perl.kit01.Z
perl.kit02.Z
perl.kit03.Z
perl.kit04.Z
perl.kit05.Z
perl.kit06.Z
perl.kit07.Z
<Currently 44 kits are available>

<Use the **get** command to get all the kits you need. Then use the **uncompress** and **tar** commands to prepare the files for compilation>

ftp> **get perl.kit01.Z**
200 PORT command successful.
150 Opening BINARY mode data connection for perl.kit01.Z (24596
bytes).
226 Transfer complete.
local: perl.kit01.Z remote: perl.kit01.Z
24596 bytes received in 32 seconds (0.75 Kbytes/s)
<Once you have all the files you need, you must disconnect from the
remote host>
ftp> **quit**
221 Goodbye.

The **mget** command can also be used to get multiple files. For example, from the **ftp** prompt to obtain all the perl kits, type the following:

ftp> **mget ***

To copy files from your local machine to a remote host, at the **ftp** prompt, type the following:

ftp> **put mylocalfile**

The **mput** command performs the same function as the **mget** command, except it copies multiple files from a local machine to the remote.

10.16 THE TELNET COMMAND

The **telnet** command allows the user to log into a remote host. The **ftp** command only allows the user to copy files, whereas the **telnet** command actually allows the user to connect and log into the remote host to execute commands. However, because this command is used by users to connect to remote hosts on the Internet, the account that is used always must have a password. Even if the user knows of an account on a remote system that does not contain a password, the **telnet** command will not allow the user to successfully connect (log in). The following example shows the **telnet** command connecting to a machine called **john**:

% **telnet john**
Trying 148.140.16.239 ...
Connected to john.COM.
Escape character is '^]'.
SunOS UNIX (john)
login: Login timed out after 60 seconds
Connection closed by foreign host.

Notice that because I did not provide an input (name for **login**), the **telnet** program disconnected my session from the remote host john. The next problem you may encounter with **telnet** is that the remote host does not allow you to successfully log in. In this case, you need to use the^] (**control** and **]**) keys together to obtain the **telnet** prompt and obtain help, as follows:

```
login: jfjklf
Password:
Login incorrect
login: <must use ^] to obtain the telnet prompt>
telnet> help
Commands may be abbreviated.  Commands are:
close        close current connection
display       display operating parameters
mode          try to enter line-by-line or character-at-a-time mode
open          connect to a site
quit        exit telnet
send          transmit special characters ('send ?' for more)
set        set operating parameters ('set ?' for more)
status        print status information
toggle         toggle operating parameters ('toggle ?' for more)
z           suspend telnet
?           print help information
telnet> quit
Connection closed.
```

chapter 11 ▶

Practical Extraction
and Report Language (PERL)

UNIX system administrators were once thought to be the primary users of PERL; however, that is no longer the case. PERL has now been used by software developers and QA and technical support engineers for a variety of applications. Many other UNIX users also have embraced the power and flexibility of PERL. The PERL programming language is a mixture of shell and C combined with the power of **awk, grep,** and **sed.**

The PERL programming language provides the following services (and more):

- The **print** comand
- Printing the contents of a file
- Formatting output with **printf**
- Arrays
- Associative arrays
- The **opendir, readdir,** and **stat** commands
- The command line

- Filters and redirection
- The **for** command
- Using the Argument Vector Variable (**ARGV**)
- The **getopts** function

11.1   THE PRINT COMMAND

The **print** command prints the contents of a variable or a string literal or both. A string literal is enclosed inside double quotes and a variable name starts with a dollar sign. PERL also supports array variables that must start with the at sign, "@". The following program displays the current date and time:

```
#!/bin/perl
$date='date';
print "The date and time is ",$date,"\n";
```

The first line tells the UNIX shell that this program is to be executed as a PERL program. The second statement is an assignment to the string variable "$date" of the result of executing the **date** command. The backquotes, or grave marks, work the same as with the shell (execute the command and provide the results as a string literal or as if the results are enclosed within double quotes). Notice that the variable name always includes the dollar sign in PERL. This is different from the shell, because the Bourne and C shell's only require the dollar sign when the contents of a variable are to be used, not the variable name itself. The last line prints a string literal ("The date and time is") followed by the contents of the variable "$date". The commas are important to separate variables from string literals. The last string literal "\n" produces a carriage-return new-line after the output is displayed. Finally, each statement must be terminated by a semicolon (as is the case in the C programming language).

As is the case with all UNIX shell scripts, PERL scripts must be executable using the **chmod** command after the program text has been entered using the **vi** editor:

```
% chmod +x myfile
% myfile
The date and time is Tue Jan 3 10:17:53 PST 1995
```

> **Exercise 1**
>
> 1 Create your own version of the **myfile** program and display the date and time followed by your system host name on the same line (use the UNIX **hostname** command to print your **hostname**).
>
> 2 Add another print statement to output the type of data presented on the first row followed by the actual data on the second row. *Hint*: Use the "\t" format to place tabs between the **date** and **hostname** output. The program should now have three lines of output.

11.2 PRINTING THE CONTENTS OF A FILE

PERL provides several functions (like the C programming language) to expedite the construction of a program. For example, to print the contents of the Message Of The Day (**/etc/motd**), the following PERL script can be created:

```
#!/bin/perl
open(MOTD,"/etc/motd");
while (<MOTD>) {
print;
}
```

After the file is made executable using the **chmod** command, the following output is displayed (depending on the contents of the **motd** file):

% myfile2
Welcome to the UNIX Operating System

In the previous example, the **open** function is used to open the file **/etc/ motd** and assign a filehandle. The **while** statement tells the print command to display each line of text until the End Of File (EOF) is encountered. It is very important to enclose the **print** statement within braces after the **while** statement. Also, note that the **while** statement does not have a semicolon at the end; otherwise, the **print** statement would never be executed.

Exercise 2

1 Create a program to open the **/etc/group** file and print each line of text.

2 Does it matter what name you use for a filehandle?

11.3   FORMATTING OUTPUT WITH PRINTF

The **print** command provides basic printing capability that is similar in nature to the **echo** command in a shell script. For more advanced formatting, the **printf** function can be used (again from the C programming language). Unlike the **print** function, **printf** requires a format specifier first followed by a variable. Notice what happens when we attempt to provide more that one format specification in double quotes (the second is ignored):

```
#!/bin/perl
$a=1;
$b=2;
printf "The value of a = %s ",$a," b = %s\n",$b;
```

```
% myfile3
The value of a = 1 %
```

The following example uses the **printf** the correct way by combining all format specifications first, followed by variables to be printed:

```
#!/bin/perl
$a=1;
$b=2;
printf "The value of a = %s b = %s\n",$a,$b;
```

```
% myfile4
The value of a = 1 b = 2
```

The **printf** function formats strings using the "%s" specifier. Many other specifiers are available (here are just a few):

%d (integer)
%.2f (floating point with two digits after the decimal point)
%x (hexadecimal—base-16 notation)
%o (octal—base-8 notation)
%e (scientific notation)
%-number (left justified number of spaces)
%number (right justified number of spaces)

The following example PERL script demonstrates the use of each format specifier defined before:

```
#!/bin/perl
printf "Integer number in decimal %d\n", 5500;
printf "Floating-point number two decimal places %.2f\n", 5500;
printf "Hexadecimal number %x\n", 5500;
printf "Octal number %o\n", 5500;
printf "Scientific number %e\n", 5500;
printf "Left justified integer number 10 spaces |%-10d|\n", 5500;
printf "Right justified integer number 10 spaces |%10d|\n", 5500;
printf qq/That is all for now\a\n/;
```

% myfile5
Integer number in decimal 5500
Floating-point number two decimal places 5500.00
Hexadecimal number 157c
Octal number 12574
Scientific number 5.500000e+03
Left justified integer number 10 spaces |5500 |
Right justified integer number 10 spaces | 5500|
That is all for now

The last line displays a beep and prints the string "That is all for now". The **qq/** is the start of a set of double quotes that is terminated by the last /. The string **q/something/** can be used for single quotes. The string **qx/date/** is the same as **'date'**, which executes the command and provides the output as a string literal. The **\a** provides an audible sound or beep. There are many other characters that also can be used. For example, **\t** provides a tab space to the right for indentation.

Exercise 3

Write a PERL script that displays your current process id in the following formats: decimal, floating-point (three decimal places), string, octal, hexadecimal, and scientific.

11.4   ARRAYS

Arrays are special variables that can contain a list or vector of values. An array variable is created by using the @ sign in front of the variable name, instead of the dollar sign, which is used to hold a single value. This is also sometimes known as a *scalar variable* (because only one value can be represented at a time). The following program assigns five names to a variable called "students". The **split** function is required to separate each name into a separate *token*. Each token collectively is then combined to create an array called "@students". Arrays in PERL always start with the subscript zero or [0], as is the case with the C programming language:

```
#!/bin/perl
$students="joe mary peter paul george";
@students=split(' ',$students);
print "The contents of the complete array is @students\n";
print "The first name was ", $students[0], "\n";
print "The second name was ", $students[1], "\n";
print "The third name was ", $students[2], "\n";
print "The fourth name was ", $students[3], "\n";
print "The fifth name was ", $students[4], "\n";
```

```
% myfile6
The contents of the complete array is joe mary peter paul george
The first name was joe
The second name was mary
The third name was peter
The fourth name was paul
The fifth name was george
```

Exercise 4

1 Assign five names to an array variable.

2 Display each name on a separate line.

3 Print each name in reverse order.

11.5 ASSOCIATIVE ARRAYS

One of the more powerful features of PERL is the use of associative arrays. With an associative array, a key can be bound or associated with each element (member) in the array. Therefore, instead of having to use a subscript or number to index to the appropriate array element, a name or key value can be used. In the following program, an associative array of dollars to gifts is provided. The user is requested to enter the approximate cost (the associative key) and the gift that can be purchased will be displayed:

```
#!/bin/perl
%array = (
 '10','some magazines',
 '20','a discounted book',
 '100','an expensive book',
 '1500','a nice computer',
 '20000','a nice car',
);
print "Enter the cost of a gift\n";
$cost=<STDIN>;
chop($cost);
foreach $price (sort keys(%array)) {
 if ($cost == $price) {
 print "You can buy ", $array{$cost}, "\n";
 }
}

% myfile7
Enter the cost of a gift
10
You can buy some magazines
```

When I entered the value 10, the program responded with a message stating what I could buy. However, when an input is provided to this program that is not equal to either 10, 20, 100, 1500 or 20000, no message is displayed:

% myfile7
5

%

It is also important to note that the **chop** function is required to remove the new-line character from the input; otherwise, the **if** statement does not match the key value that is stored in the variable "$price" to the input variable called "$cost". The **foreach** directive is a way to loop through each value in the array and assign each key to the variable "$price". Once we have a match, the message is printed.

Exercise 5

1 Create an associative array with keys for each day of the week (i.e., 0, 1, 2, 3, 4, 5, 6, where 0 is Sunday).

2 Bind a constant value to each key (day of the week) that is meaningful (useful) to you (i.e., 1—staff meeting with the boss).

3 Now, have the program determine the current day of the week using the **date** program and display the appropriate value in the associative array based on this key. In other words, if the date program says that it is Monday, the PERL program will display your string for that particular day (e.g., "staff meeting with the boss"). *Hint*: Use the **w** option to the **date** command.

11.6   THE OPENDIR, READDIR, AND STAT COMMANDS

The PERL programming language provides many functions that are not available with standard UNIX shell scripts. Therefore, PERL allows the software developer to write extensive programs using standard functions for improved code reuse. Because PERL does not require a compiler (in the strict sense, as is the case with the C language), the source is always available for easy maintenance and modification. A plethora of functions are available with PERL and this almost completely elminates having to use C whenever an operating system service, such as **read**, **open**, and **close**, is required. The **opendir** function, for example, opens a directory and returns a filehandle (the first argument to the function). The **read-dir** function stores the contents of a directory in an array after it has been succesfully opened and a valid directory filehandle has been provided. The following program displays the contents of the parent working directory. Notice that the **system** function is used to print the current working directory and display the results as a final step. This program can be modified to request any directory name as input instead:

```perl
#!/bin/perl
opendir(DIR,"..");
@parenfiles=readdir(DIR);
close(DIR);
print "The contents of the parent directory is:\n";
foreach $file ( @parenfiles ) {
 print "$file\n";
}
print "The current working directory is:\n";
system("pwd");
```

% **myfile8**
The contents of the parent directory is:
.

..
ch3
ch4
ch5
ch1
ch2
The current working directory is:
/home/rodney

The **stat** function returns a 13-element array giving the statistics for a file, directory, or special file. The **stat** function is typically used to provide a structure that contains the following information:

(device name, inode number, mode, number of links, uid, gid, raw device, size, access time, modification time, ctime, block size, number of blocks) = stat($filename);

If **stat** is passed the special filehandle consisting of an underline, no **stat** is done, but the current contents of the **stat** structure from the last **stat** or filetest are returned. The following example checks that the variable $file is executable and on a NFS mounted file system because the return is less than zero:

```
if (-x $file && (($DIR) = stat(_)) && $DIR < 0) {
    print "$file is executable NFS file\n";
}
```

Exercise 6

1 Modify the preceding program to ask the user to provide a directory name (either absolute or relative path) to open.

2 Make sure that the name provided is a valid (executable) directory. Display the contents of the directory; otherwise, provide a usage message and exit.

11.7   THE COMMAND LINE

It is possible to execute PERL commands directly from the UNIX shell prompt. For example, the following command prints each line in the **/etc/passwd** file that contains the string "sh":

% perl -ne 'print if /sh/;' /etc/passwd

Alternatively, you request that PERL print lines that do not contain a particular string. The following example displays all lines in the **/etc/group** file that do not contain the string "root":

% perl -ne 'print unless /root/' /etc/group

The following two examples search the **/etc/passwd** file for the string "rodney". If a match is found, all characters will be printed in all uppercase letters. The first example performs this function from the command line only:

% perl -ne 'tr/a-z/A-Z/;print if /RODNEY/;' /etc/passwd

The second example performs the same task; however, only the first field in the file (the user's name) is converted and printed using uppercase letters. Note that the colon is used to separate fields in the database file **names**. This special character is used by the **split** command to build an array of values in the "@line" variable:

```
#!/bin/perl
open(FILE,"names");
while (<FILE>) {
    @line=split(/:/);
    if (/rodney/) {
        print qq/\U$line[0]\n/;
    }
}
```

The next example searches the **/etc/passwd** file for the string "rodney" and change the name to "jonathan":

% perl -ne 's/rodney/jonathan/; print' /etc/passwd

Exercise 7

1 Enter the appropriate PERL command from the shell prompt to list all users in the **passwd** file that are using the **csh**.

2 Enter the PERL command from the shell to translate all data in the **/etc/passwd** file from uppercase to lowercase.

3 Write a PERL script to **print** only the user name and **login** shell from the **passwd** file. Use a tab between values.

11.8 FILTERS AND REDIRECTION

The **open** function provides the ability to **open** a file with either input or output filtering using the shell pipe facility. Input and output file redirection is also possible with the **open** function in PERL. For example, to list the contents of the current working directory and **sort** the output in reverse order, the

following program can be used (only entries that have read and write permission are displayed):

```
#!/bin/perl
open (files,"ls | sort -r |") | | die "Can't open directory: $! \n";
while (<files>) {
print if -r $file && -w $file;
}
```

Exercise 8

1 Copy the **/etc/passwd** file to your home directory and call the file **mypasswd.**

2 Create a PERL program using the **open** function to **sort** the contents of the **mypasswd** database in reverse numeric order based on the third field in the file (i.e., UID). *Hint*: See the **man** page for the **sort** command.

3 Use the **open** function; however, this time redirect the output to a file called **myoutput** and to the display.

11.9   THE EVAL FUNCTION

The **eval** function is used to evaluate the contents of the expression that is provided. The following program prompts for two numbers (integers). It then determines the remainder (modulo) of the two numbers. Finally, the program asks the user to guess the remainder; if the answer is correct, it will terminate. If the number entered is incorrect; it will loop and ask the user to guess again; if the user does not want to guess again (enters a value other than "Y"), the program will terminate:

```
#!/bin/perl
@INC="/usr/local/lib/perl";
$true=1;
$answer="Y";
print "Please enter an integer: ";
$first_integer=<STDIN>;
```

```perl
if (($first_integer <= 0) || ($first_integer >= 32767)) {
    die "Please enter a number > 0 and < 32767" ;
}
print "Please enter another integer: ";
$second_integer=<STDIN>;
if (($second_integer <= 0) || ($first_integer >= 32767)) {
    die "Please enter a number > 0 and < 32767";
}
eval{ $result = $first_integer%$second_integer; };
while ("$answer" eq "Y") {
  print "Enter your guess for the answer: ";
$guess=<STDIN>;
  if ($guess == $result) {
      print "Congratulations you guessed correctly\n";
      exit;
  }
  print "Sorry wrong answer. Want to try again? (Y) ";
  chop($answer=<STDIN>);
}
```

Exercisise 9

1 Create your own program that prompts for two input values.

2 Ask the user to guess the result of multiplying the first number by the second.

3 If the two inputs do not agree with the guess, ask again for the correct value. If the user wants to try again, make sure they enter a "y" or "Y".

11.10 THE FOR COMMAND

Looping is an important function for any programming language. PERL provides many looping constructs. In the previous example, the **while** loop was used to continue looping until a condition was no longer true. The **for** command uses a counter to determine the number of iterations to use for looping. Three values are assigned, starting, ending, and interval between each iteration. The following program demonstrates how we can specify all odd numbers starting from

92 to 2. Each time through the loop, we decrement the counter by 2 to avoid using any even numbers (prime numbers can only be divided by 1):

```perl
#!/usr/local/bin/perl
@INC="/usr/local/lib/perl";
# Program to compute all prime numbers less than 100.
# A prime number is an integer not divisible by any integer
# other than 1.
$flag=0;
print "Prime numbers between 1 and 100\n";
for ($i=97; $i>1; $i -= 2) {
    for ($j=$i-1; $j>1; $j--) {
        if (!($result = $i%$j)) {
            $flag=1;
        }
    }
    if ($flag == 0) {
        print "$i\n";
    }
    $flag=0;
}
```

Exercise 10

Create a program that solicits input from the user until no more input is to be entered by the user (i.e., a Q is entered on a line by itself) or a maximum of 100 lines has been reached. Use a **for** loop to calculate the total number of lines entered and display this number before the program completes (in either case).

11.11 USING THE ARGUMENT VECTOR VARIABLE (ARGV)

Just like in the C programming language, PERL provides a built-in variable, the ARGument Vector variable, (**ARGV**), that contains the list of arguments provided to a PERL program. The following program expects the user to provide a file as an argument. The program then determines the total number of lines in the file (same as the, word count, **wc**, program):

```perl
#!/usr/local/bin/perl
@INC="/usr/local/lib/perl";
```

```
# Program to print the line count for the file(s)
# specified as command-line arguments (w/o wc -l command).
if (!$ARGV[0]) { die "usage: program filename"; }
$i=0;
foreach $file (@ARGV) {
    open(FD,"$file");
    while (<FD>) {
        $count++;
    }
    close(FD);
    print "Line count for $file is ", $count, "\n";
    $count=0;
}
```

11.12 THE GETOPTS FUNCTION

The next example is a more comprehensive version of the previous program. This version can provide data for the total number of lines (-l) or the total number of words (-w) in a file using the **getopts** function.

```
#!/usr/local/bin/perl
@INC="/usr/local/lib/perl";
# Modified version of previous program to print words (-w) and
# lines (-l) using getopts function.
if (!$ARGV[0]) { die "usage program -w -l filename"; }
$state=0;
$count=0;
$wcount=0;
require "getopts.pl";
&Getopts('wl');
if ($opt_l) {
    foreach $file (@ARGV) {
        open(F,$file) || die "Can't open file.\n";
        while (<F>) {
            $count++;
        }
        print "$file ", $count, " lines\n";
        $count=0;
    }
}
if ($opt_w) {
    foreach $file (@ARGV) {
```

```
open(F,$ARGV[0]) || die "Can't open file.\n";
        while (<F>) {
                @array=split(/\w+/);
                $wcount += $#array;
        }
        print "$file ", $wcount, " words \n";
        $wcount=0;
    }
}
```

11.13 TESTING FILE TYPES

The following program shows how to print the modification time for all files located in a directory passed as an argument (the program name is **modtimes**).

```
#!/usr/local/bin/perl
@INC="/usr/local/lib/perl";
# Print the names of all text files in a
# directory and their modification times in days.
if (!$ARGV[0]) { die "usage: modtimes directory"; }
foreach $dirname (@ARGV) {
    open(F,"ls $dirname |") || die "Can't open directory";
    while (<F>) {
      $filename= $_;
      chop($filename);
      next unless -T $filename;
      $modtime = -M $filename;
      printf ("File %s Modification %d\n",$filename, $modtime);
}}
```

Exercise 11

1 Determine the oldest file in your current working directory. What command can you use to verify the results of your program?

2 Write a different program to determine the newest file in your current working directory.

Answers

A.1 CHAPTER 1

Exercise 1: Use the following commands to display your current shell: **set,**
printenv, echo $SHELL, or **echo $shell**.

Exercise 2: **pwd** prints the current working directory. Type **cd ..** to change to
the parent working directory and **pwd** to identify the parent
working directory (the new current working directory).

Exercise 3: Type **cd /tmp** to change directories using an absolute path. Type
cd ../etc to change to the **/etc** directory with an absolute path. An
absolute path always starts from the root (has a leading **/**). If you
are copying files to tape using the **tar** command, you may want
to use a relative path so you can extract the files from tape to a
different location on a different machine (e.g., **tar cvf /dev/rst0**
.).

Exercise 4: **ls**
touch myfile

ls -l
touch myfile
ls -l

Exercise 5:   ed myfile a <enter text> .

Exercise 6:   touch newfile
rm newfile
ls newfile
Error message is returned from the **rm** command (file does not exist). touch newfile
rm /home/rodney/newfile

Exercise 7:   touch "?special_file"
rm "?special_file"
touch spring fling wing
ls *ing
rm ?ing
The question mark matches just one character. The asterisk matches multiple characters. In this case, **rm *ing** removes spring fling wing.

A.2   CHAPTER 2

Exercise 1:   who
who > outputdata

Exercise 2:   mail rodney <text entered and terminated with a ^D on a line by itself>
mail <use **s** command while reading a mail message>
ed <inside of the editor 1,$s/^/>/ after deleting header>

Exercise 3:   man man
man -k searching
apropos searching

Exercise 4:   echo "rodney"
set last="wilson" <csh only>
echo $last
set student="wilson"
echo $student
echo student <the variable name>

Exercise 5:   date

Exercise 6:   touch
time sleep 5

Exercise 7:   mv
yes.
no.
touch new
mv new new1
ls new <file not found>
mv new1 new1 <files are identical>

Exercise 8:   lpr and lp
lpq and lpstat

Exercise 9:   grep "The" *
grep "The day" *

Exercise 10:   head big
tail big
wc bigfile

Exercise 11:   sort myfile
sort -nr bigfile

Exercise 12:   diff a b
sort a > c
diff a c
No output is provided by the **diff** command when two identical files are provided as input. The **sdiff** command provides a side-by-side difference and is useful to see specific line differences.

A.3   CHAPTER 3

Exercise 1:   mkdir
yes.
Permission denied message.
Permission denied message again.
Permission denied message.
Permission denied because the directory cannot be removed if it contains other files.

Exercise 2:   cp, touch or ed

```
chmod 777 newfile
ls -l
chmod 600 newfile
chmod u+rwx,g+r-wx,o+r-wx newfile
umask 066
```

Exercise 3:
```
ln newfile linkfile
ls -i newfile linkfile
ln -s newfile /tmp/newfile
```

A.4   CHAPTER 4

Exercise 1:   stty or stty -a
stty erase ^H
I really used the backspace key after I typed **stty erase**; however, the shell already mapped that key to a ^H sequence. (You can also type the caret, "^", followed by a capital H.) This is useful if you already have the control H key mapped to another function.

Exercise 2:
```
sh
set or echo $PATH
PATH=$PATH:/tmp
export PATH
echo "date" > myfile
chmod 755 myfile
mv myfile /tmp
which myfile
cd /
myfile
yes.
```

Exercise 3:   PS1='whoami'" "
There are many ways to perform this task. One way is to simply assign it your name (i.e., **PS2=rodney**). The problem with this method is that its assignment is not variable (i.e., it is not correct for users other than rodney). For example, what if we wanted the name to change depending upon our log in name. In UNIX, we can use the **su** (substitute user) command to log in with a new user name.
PS2="second prompt> "

Exercise 4:   ls > lsfile
date >> lsfile
Permission denied.

Exercise 5:   mail rodney < /etc/group
mail
mail -s "The motd file" rodney < /etc/motd

Exercise 6:   ls -lR | tee /dev/tty | lpr
ls -lR [a-p]* | tee /dev/tty | lpr

Exercise 7:   cp /etc/termcap bigfile
diff /etc/termcap bigfile
sum bigfile; sum /etc/termcap
vi myfile (^Z in the middle of editor)
echo "Want to go to lunch" | mail rodney
fg

Exercise 8:   ls [b-j]*
ls [w-p]
ls *[l-p]
ls [b-jl-p]*

Exercise 9:   cp /etc/passwd mypasswd
grep \^root mypasswd
grep \$sh mypasswd
grep '[A-P]' *
grep \^`whoami` mypasswd
tr '[p-z][P-Z]' mypasswd

A.5   CHAPTER 5

Exercise 1:   ya and pu
n
q!
- + <cr>
ex -r <file name as stated in mail message>

Exercise 2:   i a o Left and right
$
^
:set showmode
x dw dd
d$

Exercise 3: /string
n
N
?string
1,$s/oldstring/newstring/g

Exercise 4: :r !date
<position to last line> :r !date (repeat last command)

Exercise 5: :w! /tmp/yourname
~

Exercise 6: ksh
set -o vi (must then use <esc> key
<esc> then hjkl keys to reposition to a command, then i a dw cw

A.6 CHAPTER 6

Exercise 1: cd /tmp
tar cf - . | (cd; tar xf - .)
Command subgrouping ensures that our home directory (in this case) remains as the destination directory during extraction (writing).
Otherwise, the data from /tmp are written to our original working directory where we first started the command, not our home directory.

Exercise 2: ls > /tmp/testfile
sjfklsj > myerrors 2>&1
fjfjf >> myerrors 2>&1

Exercise 3: echo "The date is" `date`
echo "My name is" `whoami`

Exercise 4: #!/bin/sh
echo "Enter your log in name"
read name
realname=`whoami`
if test "$name" = "$realname"
then
    echo "success"
else
    echo "failure"
fi

Exercise 5:
```
#!/bin/sh
for file in `ls [a-qw-z]*`
do
    echo "$file"
done
#!/bin/sh
for file in `ls [a-qw-z]*`
do
    rm -i "$file"
done
```

Exercise 6:
```
#!/bin/sh
while true
do
    echo "Enter a directory name"
    read name
    if test "$name" = "$HOME"
    then
            exit
    fi
done
```

Exercise 7:
```
username=`whoami`
echo $username
unset username or username=""
```

Exercise 8:
```
expr
#!/bin/sh
count=0
while true
do
    echo "Enter a directory name"
    read name
    if test "$name" = "$HOME"
    then
            exit
    else
            count=`expr $count + 1`
    fi
done
```

Exercise 9:
```
#!/bin/sh
echo "Enter a command line option"
read option
case "$option" in
```

```
    l)
        ls
    p)
        pwd
    w)
        whoami
    *)
        echo "Invalid command request"
    esac
```

Exercise 10:
```
shift
#!/bin/sh
set a b c d e f g h i j k l
while [ $# -gt 0]
do
    if test $# -eq 10 -o $# -eq 11
    then
        echo $*
    fi
done
```

Exercise 11:
```
#!/bin/sh
print_function()
{
    pwd
    echo $PS1
    echo $PS2
    echo $PATH
    echo $USER
}
print_function
#!/bin/sh
print_function_detail()
{
echo "The current directory is " 'pwd'
echo "The primary prompt is "$PS1
echo "The secondary prompt is " $PS2
echo "The search path for commands is "$PATH
echo "My user name is "$USER
}
print_function_detail
```

Exercise 12:
```
#!/bin/sh
trap continue 2
```

```
while true
do
    echo "Enter the user's name"
    read name
    echo "Enter the user's phone number"
    read phone
    echo "Enter the user's fax number"
    read fax
    echo $name $phone $fax >> employee_info
    echo "Do you want to continue? (n/N)"
    read answer
    if [ "$answer" = "n" -o "$answer" = "N" ]
    then
        exit
    fi
done
```
Other signals may include SIGHUP "1", SIGQUIT "3", and SIG-ILL "4".

A.7 CHAPTER 7

Exercise 1:   set history=100
!l
<type **history** and find the command number>
!-2

Exercise 2:   **write joedoe | | echo "joedoe not logged in" | mail rodney**

Exercise 3:   Use single or double quotes (except for the **history** character) or the \ character.
touch "?mark"
rm "?mark"
echo "My log in name is " `whoami`

Exercise 4:   **alias lr ls -R**
alias lrm ls | more
alias cd   cd \!*; set prompt=`hostname`":"`pwd`

Exercise 5:   #!/bin/csh
start:
echo "Enter your name and home phone number "
set user_info = $<

```
echo "Your name and number is"
echo $user_info
echo "Enter y if this is correct"
set answer = $<
if "$answer" != "y" then
   goto start
else
   echo "user_info" >> ~rodney/userdata
endif
```

Other information to solicit can include the user's system used for backup, critical mount points (file systems), projects and project status, etc.

Exercise 6:
```
#!/bin/csh
foreach file ('ls ')
   echo -n "Do you want to create a backup of $file?"
   set answer = $<
   if "$answer" == "y" then
      cp $file $file.bak
   endif
end
#!/bin/csh -x
set input=""
while ( "$input" != "n")
     echo "Enter a line of input"
     set input = $<
     echo $input >> output
end
cat output
```

Exercise 7:
```
cp myfile newfile
vi newfile
^newfile^afile
!cp:p
^newfile^bfile
```

A.8   CHAPTER 8

Exercise 1:   Assuming all home directories are located under /home: **du -s / home | sort -nr**
du | sort -nr

Exercise 2:   find. find / -name "*" -print
```
#!/bin/sh
find /home/rodney \(-type f -size 0 -o -name "core" \) -ok rm {} \;
find /home/rodney -name "*.o" -ok rm {} \;
```

Exercise 3:   sed '1,5d' junkfile > mailfile
sed '1,$s/^/>/' mailfile > mailfile
sed '1,$s/^>//' mailfile > mailfile
sed 'w /tmp/sed.exercise' myfile

Exercise 4:   cp /etc/passwd mypasswd
awk '{print}' mypasswd
awk -F: '!($2 == "") {print}' mypasswd
cp /etc/shadow myshadow (Use **myshadow** instead of **mypasswd**.)
```
#!/bin/sh
awk -F: '!($2 == "") {print $1}' mypasswd >> users
for i in 'cat users'
do
    echo "You don't have a have password" | mail $i
done
awk -F: 'BEGIN{FS=":";OFS="\t"; \
print "\t Login Name \t Comment \t Home \t Default Shell"; \
print ""} \
{printf "\t %-6x \t %-20s \t %-10s \t %-10s\n",$1,$5,$6,$7}'
mypasswd
```

A.9   CHAPTER 9

Exercise 1:   **cc myfile.c**
man cc
cc myfile.c -o myprog

Exercise 2:   # Makefile
CC=cc
SOURCES=myfile.c
OBJECTS=myfile.o
myprog: $(OBJECTS)
$(CC) -o $@ $(OBJECTS)
myprog.o: myprog.c
$(CC) -c myprog.c

```
make -f mymakefile
clean:
    rm *.o myprog a.out
```

Exercise 3:

```
mkdir RCS
ci myfile.c (insert comments)
co -l myfile.c
su joe (or any other user)
co -l myfile (already locked by user xxx message is displayed)
rlog RCS/*
```

Exercise 4:

```
myname()
{
        system("whoami");
}
cc -c myname.c
ar cr mylibrary.a myname.o
ranlib mylibrary.a
yes.
main()
{
myname();
}
cc test1.c mylibrary.a -o test1
test1
```

A.10   CHAPTER 10

Exercise 1:   tar cvf /dev/rfd0 . (Assumes the floppy disk is formatted and is not write protected.)
tar cvf /dev/rst0 . (Assumes the tape is inserted and is not write protected.)
tar cvf mybackup.tar .
tar tvf mybackup.tar (Will list contents of tar archive backup.)
mv myfile dummy
tar xvf mybackup.tar ./myfile
diff myfile dummy or **sum myfile sum dummy** or **cmp myfile dummy**

Exercise 2:   find . -depth -print | cpio -o > /dev/rfd0
find . -depth -print | cpio -o > /dev/rst1

Exercise 3:
```
dd if=/dev/null of=empty_file count=1 bs=512
ls -l empty_file or du empty_file
dd if=mypasswd conv=swab
```

Exercise 4:
```
useradd -s /bin/csh test
useradd -s /bin/printer.script printer
#!/bin/sh
trap continue 2
lpc restart
exit
# End printer.script file
chmod 4755 /etc/printer.script
```

Exercise 5:
```
lpr myfile.c
lp myfile.c
lpq and lpstat
cancel <jobnumber> <printername>
reject -r "Printer is currently unavailable" lp
```

Exercise 6:
```
du -s /home
df
```
Request users backup and/or remove old files.
Prune old **core** files (see the previous chapter's exercise with the **find** command).

Exercise 7:
```
fdformat (SUN machines) or format (others)
mkfs /dev/rfd0
mkdir /floppy (Must be root)
mount /dev/fd0 /floppy (Must be root)
cp *.c /floppy
umount /floppy
volcheck
```

Exercise 8:
```
find / -name "core" -mtime 30+ -print >> /tmp/corefiles
echo "See the file /tmp/corefiles for all files that will be
removed in 2 weeks" | mail allusers
```
Process accounting files, old object files, duplicate files, etc.

Exercise 9:
```
sh or xclock& many others
kill process-id or kill job-number (C shell only)
ps (shows only our processes)
```
Use script in Chapter 6 (Exercise 12) or other scripts with trap handlers.
You must use a signal other than 2 to terminate this process.

Exercise 10:
```
crontab -e
```

0 2 * * 1,2,3,4,5 /home/rodney/mybackup
0 2 * * 1,2,3,4,5 /home/rodney/mybackup > /home/rodney/
backup_errors 2>&1
Redirection is important so you can monitor error messages that
might occur during the backup process. There is no output terminal (display device) assigned (dedicated) to any **cron** jobs.

A.11 CHAPTER 11

Exercise 1:
```
#!/bin/perl
$date='date';
$myhost='hostname';
print "The date and time is ", $date, "My host is ", $myhost,"\n";
print "The date and time", "My hostname\n";
print $date, $myhost,"\n";
```

Exercise 2:
```
#!/bin/perl
open(GROUP, "/etc/group");
while (<GROUP>) {
    print;
}
```
No, only that you reference the same name in the **while** loop that
was used to **open** the file name **/etc/group**.

Exercise 3:
Obtain our current process id using **'echo $$'**
```
#!/bin/perl
$pid='echo $$';
printf "Decimal output %d\n", $pid;
printf "Floating-point output %.3f\n", $pid;
printf "String output %s\n", $pid;
printf "Octal output %o\n", $pid;
printf "Hexadecimal output %x\n", $pid;
printf "Scientific output %e\n", $pid;
```

Exercise 4:
```
#!/bin/perl
@names="joe mary bill nancy frank";
@name=split(' ',$names[0]);
print $name[0],"\n";
print $name[1],"\n";
print $name[2],"\n";
print $name[3],"\n";
```

```perl
print $name[4],"\n";
#Now print in reverse order (could also do this with a for loop)
print $name[4],"\n";
print $name[3],"\n";
print $name[2],"\n";
print $name[1],"\n";
print $name[0],"\n";
```

Exercise 5:

```perl
#!/bin/perl
%array = (
'1','Monday - staff meeting with Fred',
'2','Tuesday - group meeting',
'3','Wednesday - presentation on metrics',
'4','Thursday - status report due',
'5','Friday - dress down day',
'6','Saturday - teach classes',
'0','Sunday - see wife again',
);
$day='date "+%w"';
chop($day);
foreach $key (values(%array)) {
   if ($count eq $day) {
      print "$array$key\n";
   }
   $count++;
}
```

Exercise 6:

```perl
#!/bin/perl
print "Enter a directory name \n";
$dir=<STDIN>;
chop($dir);
if (-x $dir) {
     open(DIR,"ls $dir |") || die "Could not open directory";
}
print "The contents of the directory:\n";
     while (<DIR>) {
          $path = $_;
          chop($path);
          print "$path\n";
     }
print "The current working directory is:\n";
system("pwd");
close(DIR);
```

Exercise 7:

```
perl -ne 'print if /csh/;' /etc/passwd
perl -ne 'tr/A-Z/a-z/;print;' /etc/passwd
#!/bin/perl
open(FILE, "/etc/passwd");
while (<FILE>) {
   @line=split(/:/);
   print $line[0], "\t", $line[6], "\n";
}
```

Exercise 8:

```
cp /etc/passwd mypasswd
#!/bin/perl
open (files,"sort -t: +2n -3 -nr mypasswd |") || die "Can't open
directory: $! \n";
while (<files>) {
   print;
}
#!/bin/perl
open (files,"sort -t: +2n -3 -nr mypasswd | tee myoutput |") ||
die "Can't open directory: $! \n";
while (<files>) {
   print;
}
```

Exercise 9:

```
#!/bin/perl
@INC="/usr/local/lib/perl";
$true=1;
$answer="Y";
print "Please enter an integer: ";
$first_integer=<STDIN>;
if (($first_integer <= 0) || ($first_integer >= 32767)) {
     die "Please enter a number > 0 and < 32767" ;
}
print "Please enter another integer: ";
$second_integer=<STDIN>;
if (($second_integer <= 0) || ($first_integer >= 32767)) {
     die "Please enter a number > 0 and < 32767";
}
eval{ $result = $first_integer*$second_integer; };
while ("$answer" eq "y" || "$answer" eq "Y") {
  print "Enter your guess for the answer: ";
$guess=<STDIN>;
  if ($guess == $result) {
     print "Congratulations you guessed correctly \n";
     exit;
```

```
                }
                print "Sorry wrong answer. Want to try again? (Y) ";
                chop($answer=<STDIN>);
        }
```

Exercise 10:
```
#!/usr/local/bin/perl
@INC="/usr/local/lib/perl";
$count=0;
print "Enter input\n";
while ($count <= 99) {
        $input=<STDIN>;
        chop($input);
        if ("$input" eq "Q") {
                print "The total number of lines entered was ",
$count,"\n";
                exit;
        }
        else {
                $count++;
        }
}
print "\n";
print "The total number of lines entered was ", $count;
```

Exercise 11:
```
#!/usr/local/bin/perl
@INC="/usr/local/lib/perl";
$newtime=1;
foreach $filename (@ARGV) {
        open(F,"ls |") || die "Can't open directory";
        while (<F>) {
                $filename= $_;
                chop($filename);
                $modtime = -M $filename;
                if ($modtime < $newtime) {
                        $newtime = $modtime;
                        $newfile = $filename
                }
        }
        printf ("Newest file is %s\n",$newfile);
}
ls -l ( shows date and time stamps)
#!/usr/local/bin/perl
@INC="/usr/local/lib/perl";
$oldtime=1;
```

```
foreach $filename (@ARGV) {
    open(F,"ls |") || die "Can't open directory";
    while (<F>) {
        $filename= $_;
        chop($filename);
        $modtime = -M $filename;
        if ($modtime > $oldtime) {
            $oldtime = $modtime;
            $oldfile = $filename
        }
    }
    printf ("Oldest file is %s \n",$oldfile);
}
```

appendix B▸

UNIX Command Reference Guide

acctcom (1)	search and print process accounting files
adb (1)	general-purpose debugger
addbib (1)	create or extend a bibliographic database
apropos (1)	locate commands by keyword lookup
arch (1)	display the architecture of the current host
as (1)	assembler
at, batch (1)	execute a command or script at a specified time
atq (1)	display the queue of jobs to be run at specified times
atrm (1)	remove jobs spooled by **at** or **batch**
awk (1)	pattern scanning and processing language
bar (1)	create tape archives and add or extract files
bc (1)	arbitrary-precision arithmetic language
biff (1)	give notice of incoming mail messages
cal (1)	display a calendar
calendar (1)	a simple reminder service
cb (1)	a simple C program beautifier

cd (1)	change working directory
checknr (1)	check **nroff** and **troff** input files; report possible errors
chgrp (1)	change the group ownership of a file
chkey (1)	create or change encryption key
clear (1)	clear the terminal screen
click (1)	enable or disable the keyboard's keystroke click
clock (1)	display the time in an icon or window
cmp (1)	perform a byte-by-byte comparison of two files
colcrt (1)	filter **nroff** output for a terminal lacking overstrike capability
coloredit (1)	alter the color map segment
colrm (1)	remove characters from specified columns within each line
comm (1)	display lines in common, and lines not in common, between two sorted lists
compress (1)	compress or expand files; display expanded contents
cp (1)	copy files
cpio (1)	copy file archives in and out
cpp (1)	the C language preprocessor
crontab (1)	install, edit, remove, or list a user's crontab file
crypt (1)	encode or decode a file
csh (1)	a shell (command interpreter) with a C-like syntax and advanced interactive features csh, %, @, alias, bg, break, breaksw, case, continue, default, dirs, else, end, endif, endsw, eval, exec, exit, fg, foreach, glob, goto, hashstat, history, if, jobs, label, limit, logout, notify, onintr, popd, pushd, rehash, repeat, set, setenv, shift, source, stop, suspend, switch, then, umask, unalias, unhash, unlimit, unset, unsetenv, while (1) - C shell built-in commands
ctags (1)	create a tags file for use with **ex** and **vi**
dbx (1)	source-level debugger
dc (1)	desk calculator
dd (1)	convert and copy files with various data formats
deroff (1)	remove **nroff**, **troff**, **tbl**, and **eqn** constructs
des (1)	encrypt or decrypt data using Data Encryption Standard
diff (1)	display line-by-line differences between pairs of text files
diffmk (1)	mark differences between versions of a **troff** input file
dis (1)	object code disassembler for Common Object File Format (COFF)
domainname (1)	set or display name of the current NIS (Network Information Service) domain
dos2unix (1)	convert text file from DOS format to ISO format
ed, red (1)	basic line editor
eject (1)	eject media device from drive
env (1)	obtain or alter environment variables for command execution

eqn, neqn (1)	typset mathematics
error (1)	categorize compiler error messages; insert at responsible source file lines
ex, edit, e (1)	line editors
expand (1)	expand TAB characters to SPACE characters and vice versa
fdformat (1)	format diskettes for use with SunOS
file (1)	determine the type of a file by examining its contents
find (1)	find files by name or by other characteristics
finger (1)	display information about users
fmt, fmt_mail (1)	simple text and mail-message formatters
fold (1)	fold long lines for display on an output device of a given width
fontedit (1)	a vfont screen-font editor
foption (1)	determine available floating-point code generation options
from (1)	display the sender and date of newly arrived mail messages
gcore (1)	get core images of running processes
getopts (1)	parse command options in shell scripts
gprof (1)	display call-graph profile data
groups (1)	display a user's group memberships
head (1)	display first few lines of specified files
hostid (1)	print the numeric identifier of the current host
hostname (1)	set or print name of current host system
indent (1)	indent and format a C program source file
indxbib (1)	create an inverted index to a bibliographic database
inline (1)	in-line procedure call expander
install (1)	install files
intro (1)	introduction to commands
ipcrm (1)	remove a message queue, semaphore set, or shared memory ID
ipcs (1)	report interprocess communication facilities status
join (1)	relational database operator
keylogin (1)	decrypt and store secret key
keylogout (1)	delete stored secret key
kill (1)	send a signal to a process or terminate a process
last (1)	indicate last login by user or terminal
lastcomm (1)	show the last commands executed, in reverse order
ld, ld.so (1)	link editor; dynamic link editor
ldd (1)	list dynamic dependencies
leave (1)	remind you when you have to leave
lex (1)	lexical analysis program generator
line (1)	read one line
logger (1)	add entries to the system log
login (1)	log in to the system
logname (1)	get the name by which you logged in

look (1)	find words in the system dictionary or lines in a sorted list
lookbib (1)	find references in a bibliographic database
lorder (1)	find an ordering relation for an object library
lp, cancel (1)	send/cancel requests to a printer
lpq (1)	display the queue of printer jobs
lpr (1)	send a job to the printer
lprm (1)	remove jobs from the printer queue
lpstat (1)	display the printer status information
lptest (1)	generate line printer ripple pattern
lsw (1)	list TFS whiteout entries
mach (1)	display the processor type of the current host machid, sun, iAPX286, m68k, pdp11, sparc, u3b, u3b2, u3b5, u3b15, vax, i386 (1) - return a true exit status if the processor is of the indicated type
mail, Mail (1)	read or send mail messages
make (1)	maintain, update, and regenerate related programs and files
man (1)	display reference manual pages; find reference pages by keyword
mesg (1)	permit or deny messages on the terminal
mkdir (1)	make a directory
mkstr (1)	create an error message file by massaging C source files
more, page (1)	browse or page through a text file
mps (1)	display the status of current processes on an MP system
mpstat (1)	show multiprocessor usage
mt (1)	magnetic tape control
mv (1)	move or rename files
nawk (1)	pattern scanning and processing language
newgrp (1)	log in to a new group
nice (1)	run a command at low priority
nm (1)	print symbol name list
nroff (1)	format documents for display or line printer
objdump (1)	dump selected parts of a COFF object file
organizer (1)	file and directory manager
pagesize (1)	display the size of a page of memory
passwd (1)	change local or NIS password information
printenv (1)	display environment variables currently set
prof (1)	display profile data
ps (1)	display the status of current processes
ptx (1)	generate a permuted index
pwd (1)	display the pathname of the current working directory
quota (1)	display a user's disk quota and usage
ranlib (1)	convert archives to random libraries
rdist (1)	remote file distribution program

refer (1)	expand and insert references from a bibliographic database
rev (1)	reverse the order of characters in each line
rm, rmdir (1)	remove (unlink) files or directories
roffbib (1)	format and print a bibliographic database
rpcgen (1)	RPC (Remote Procedure Call) protocol compiler
sccs (1)	front end for the Source Code Control System (SCCS)
sccs-admin, admin (1)	create and administer SCCS history files
sccs-cdc, cdc (1)	change the delta commentary of an SCCS delta
sccs-comb, comb (1)	combine SCCS deltas
sccs-delta, delta (1)	make a delta to an SCCS file
sccs-get, get (1)	retrieve a version of an SCCS file
sccs-help, help (1)	ask for help regarding SCCS error or warning messages
sccs-prs, prs (1)	display selected portions of an SCCS history
sccs-prt, prt (1)	display delta table information from an SCCS file
sccs-rmdel, rmdel (1)	remove a delta from an SCCS file
sccs-sact, sact (1)	show editing activity status of an SCCS file
sccs-sccsdiff, sccsdiff (1)	compare two versions of an SCCS file
sccs-unget, unget (1)	undo a previous get of an SCCS file
sccs-val, val (1)	validate an SCCS file
screenblank (1)	turn off the screen when the mouse and keyboard are idle
screendump (1)	dump a frame-buffer image to a file
screenload (1)	load a frame-buffer image from a file
script (1)	make typescript of a terminal session
sh (1)	shell, the standard UNIX system command interpreter and command-level language
size (1)	display the size of an object file
sleep (1)	suspend execution for a specified interval
soelim (1)	resolve and eliminate ".so" requests from **nroff** or **troff** input
sortbib (1)	sort a bibliographic database
spell (1)	report spelling errors
split (1)	split a file into pieces
strings (1)	find printable strings in an object file or binary
strip (1)	remove symbols from an object file
symorder (1)	rearrange a list of symbols
sync (1)	update the superblock; force changed blocks to the disk
syswait (1)	execute a command, suspending termination until user input
tail (1)	display the last part of a file
talk (1)	talk to another user
tar (1)	create tape archives and add or extract files
tbl (1)	format tables for **nroff** or **troff**
tcopy (1)	copy a magnetic tape
tcov (1)	construct test coverage analysis and statement-by-statement profile

tee (1)	replicate the standard output
trace (1)	trace system calls and signals
troff (1)	typeset or format documents
true, false (1)	provide truth values
tset, reset (1)	establish or restore terminal characteristics
tsort (1)	topological sort
tty (1)	display the name of the terminal
ul (1)	do underlining
uname (1)	display the name of the current system
uncompress (1)	compress or expand files; display expanded contents
unexpand (1)	unexpand TAB characters to SPACE characters
unifdef (1)	resolve and remove ifdef'ed lines from **cpp** input
uniq (1)	remove or report adjacent duplicate lines
units (1)	conversion program
unix2dos (1)	convert text file from ISO format to DOS format
unwhiteout (1)	remove a TFS whiteout entry
uptime (1)	show how long the system has been up
users (1)	display a compact list of users logged in
vacation (1)	reply to **mail** automatically
vfontinfo (1)	inspect and print out information about fonts
vgrind (1)	grind **nice** program listings
vi, view, vedit (1)	visual display editor based on **ex** (1)
vplot (1)	plot graphics for a Versatec printer
vswap (1)	convert a foreign font file
vtroff (1)	**troff** to a raster plotter
vwidth (1)	make a **troff** width table for a font
w (1)	who is logged in and what are they doing
wait (1)	wait for a process to finish
wall (1)	write to all users logged in
wc (1)	display a count of lines, words, and characters
what (1)	extract SCCS version information from a file
whatis (1)	display a one-line summary about a keyword
whereis (1)	locate the binary, source, and manual page files for a command
which (1)	locate a command; display its pathname or alias
who (1)	who is logged in on the system
whoami (1)	display the effective current user name
whois (1)	TCP/IP (Transmission Control Protocol/Internet Protocol) Internet user name directory service
write (1)	write a message to another user
xsend, xget, enroll (1)	send or receive secret mail
xstr (1)	extract strings from C programs to implement shared strings
yacc (1)	yet another compiler-compiler: parsing program generator

yes (1)   be repetitively affirmative (used with **fsck**)
ypcat (1)   print values in a NIS database
ypmatch (1)   print the value of one or more keys from a NIS map
yppasswd (1)   change your network password in the NIS database
ypwhich (1)   return **hostname** of NIS server or map master
zcat (1)   compress or expand files; display expanded contents

Review Questions

C.1 GETTING STARTED

1　Why does UNIX require a log in name and password?
2　What command changes your existing password?
3　What do the terms UID and GID mean? Where are they defined? When are these values established?
4　What is the difference between a file and a process?
5　What is the purpose of the UNIX shell?
6　What UNIX command shows your current working directory?
7　How can you display the contents of a directory (e.g., **/tmp**)?
8　How can you change your current working directory to **/usr/tmp**?
9　What command removes all files that start with the letter "**a**" located in the current working directory?
10　What command creates an empty file or updates the date and time stamps for an existing file?
11　How can you list all files in the current working directory that contain the string "ile"?

C.2 FILE AND DIRECTORY COMMAND QUESTIONS

1 What command displays all files and subdirectories recursively?
2 How can you list all hidden files (e.g., **.cshrc**)?
3 How can you determine the inode number for a file?
4 What command interactively deletes all file names that contain the string "junk"?
5 What command deletes a directory and all subdirectories?
6 For what purpose does UNIX provide input and output file redirection?
7 Give an example of output file redirection. How about error messages; will they also be redirected? If not, how can you also send errors to a file?
8 Give an example of input file redirection.
9 How does a pipe differ from input or output file redirection?
10 Give one example of a command pipeline.
11 What command sends output data to both a disk file called "fun_book" as well as to the standard output device (display)?
12 How can you start a program so that it runs in the background (e.g., a file copy operation)?

C.3 EDITOR QUESTIONS

1 Explain the following **vi** commands:
    (a) Move up one line
    (b) Move down one line
    (c) Move right one character
    (d) Move left one character
    (e) Read in the output of executing a shell command
    (f) Delete three lines
    (g) Delete a single character
    (h) Delete a word
    (i) Delete from the current cursor position to the end of the line
    (j) Open a new line below the current cursor position
    (k) Open a new line above the current cursor position
    (l) Add text to the right of the cursor
    (m) Add text to the left of the cursor
2 What command is used to print the contents of a file in the **ex** editor?
3 How can you copy and paste text in the **ex** editor?

C.4   THE BOURNE SHELL

1 What command(s) displays all environment variables for the Bourne shell?
2 What command displays all local variables (all shells)?
   (a) How can you assign a value to a local variable in the Bourne shell?
   (b) How can you assign a value to a local variable in the C Shell?
3 What is the purpose of the PATH environment variable?
4 What command appends to the PATH environment variable an additional directory (e.g., /tmp)?
5 Why should you consider using the **export** command afterward?
6 What special character can be used to store the results of executing a command as a string literal?
7 Why is command subgrouping important or useful?
8 Provide an example of a command subgroup.

C.5   C SHELL COMMAND QUESTIONS

1 What is the command that sets the C shell **history** buffer to 100?
2 How can you repeat the last command?
3 How can you modify the previous command?
4 Explain the purpose of the **alias** command.
5 Give an example of using the **alias** command.
6 What command appends data to an existing file called "names" when the C shell noclobber environment variable is set?
7 What command appends to the path environment variable an additional directory (e.g., /usr1)?
8 What command(s) displays all environment variables for the C shell?
9 What is the purpose of the path environment variable?
10 What is the difference between the single forward and double-quote characters?

C.6 PATTERN MATCHING AND SEARCHING COMMAND QUESTIONS

1 Create a file that contains a list of individual first names and last names separated by a space.
2 How can you use the **awk** command to print data in column 2 (last name) before column 1 (first name)?
3 What command searches for the string "UNIX" in all files in the current working directory?
4 How can you display the last 10 lines of a file without using the **tail** command?
5 What command displays all files that have not been accessed in over 20 days?
6 What command searches the **/usr** file system for users who are considered disk "hogs" (i.e., are consuming the most amount of disk space)?

C.7 BASIC COMMANDS

1 What one command is used to **mail** the **/etc/group** file to a user from the shell?
   (a) What **mail** or **mailx** command saves a message to your private mbox?
   (b) What **mail** or **mailx** command allows you to read your mail?
2 What command allows you to view the top five lines of a file?
3 What command displays the bottom 20 lines of a file?
4 What command shows you all users that are currently logged into a system?
5 How can you get more information on the **ls** command?
6 What command in UNIX can be used to rename a file?
7 How can you a link to a file that is not located on the same system or file system?
8 What command can be used to remove a directory? If the directory is not empty, can this command still be used? If not, what command can be used instead?

C.8   PROGRAMMING TOOLS QUESTIONS

1 What command is used to compile a C program?
2 What command is commonly used to clean up, build, and execute a program in the UNIX environment?
3 What commands are commonly used with the Revision Control System to change source code files?
4 What command is used to create a static library?

C.9   SYSTEM ADMINISTRATION QUESTIONS

1 Using the device name "/dev/rst1" and the **tar** command, give answers to the following questions:
   (a) Copy all the files in your current working directory to the tape device mentioned.
   (b) List all the files on the tape and store the results in a file called "tar_files".
   (c) Extract all files from the tape to the "/tmp" directory.
   (d) What kind of path name does this operation require for successful extraction for a nonroot user?
2 What command for SVR4 systems is used to add users? What is the advantage of this command over the BSD method?
3 What is the purpose of the **cron** and **at** programs?
4 What command allows you to copy a file from one host to another without having a valid log in on the remote host?
5 What command allows you to log in to a remote host connected to the Internet?
6 What files are commonly used to configure the X Window System environment?
7 What are some potential advantages of using SL/IP over **uucp**?
8 What commands are used to configure a remote printer?
9 What command can be used to mount a DOS file system on a UNIX system?

Index